CRYPTOCURRENCY

EMPOWERS

GLOBAL FINANCIAL SYSTEMS

CRYPTOCURRENCY

E M P O W E R S

GLOBAL FINANCIAL SYSTEMS

D.V. Nathan, MBA, MSc, B.A, FCIM(UK)

Archway Publishing books may be ordered
through booksellers or by contacting:

Archway Publishing
1663 Liberty Drive
Bloomington, IN 47403
www.archwaypublishing.com
844-669-3957

Because of the dynamic nature of the Internet, any web addresses or
links contained in this book may have changed since publication and may
no longer be valid. The views expressed in this work are solely those
of the author and do not necessarily reflect the views of the publisher,
and the publisher hereby disclaims any responsibility for them.

ISBN: 978-1-6657-5361-6 (sc)
ISBN: 978-1-6657-5362-3 (e)

Library of Congress Control Number: 2023922266

Print information available on the last page.

Archway Publishing rev. date: 11/28/2023

CONTENTS

FOREWORD

I have great pleasure in writing this foreword for the book 'Cryptocurrency empowers global financial system.' Congratulations to Dan Vivek Nathan on another fantastic book after publishing books on 'Global Market/Marketing Research in 21st century and beyond', and Entrepreneurship education.' Dan done it again. He has taken a wide ranging constantly evolving subject 'Cryptocurrency empowers global financial system' and made it relevant to the audience of Cryptocurrency. In terms of the global financial system, cryptocurrency is the most important technical breakthrough of this generation, and 'Cryptocurrency empowers global financial system' is the book to it, I have read it.

In today's digital world, we have seen many pedagogues' books and articles emerging on OpenAI/ChatGPT, Bard AI Chatbot, Generative AI, Magnifier etc., we have noticed a dearth of financial and investing guides covering appropriate approaches and tools for cryptocurrencies in the financial system focused on the digital space.

This book also leads the way in demonstrating that in the digital space with the new emerging decentralized system no one can stand still when it comes to global cryptocurrencies.

I have been gratified to see this book emerging as one of the first to specifically address cryptocurrency and the global financial system. The author has the uncanny ability to distill the digital world of complex information into a form that is accessible, useful, and intriguing, and I trust this book will find a particular place in the field of cryptocurrency and the global financial system for years-to-come.

A. Pritchard,
Member of The Chartered Institute of Marketing, UK,
Member of The European Marketing Confederation, Belgium

REVIEWS

Mr. Nathan uses his visionary insight and deep Knowledge to give readers an easy-to-understand, comprehensive guide on bitcoin and blockchain technology.

He offers a balanced assessment of the centralized and decentralized finance in his book. The author explores in a clear, concise manner, and easy to follow details of CBDC, Fintech, and bitcoin and blockchain technology.

Michael Huen, Chainlink Labs

Mr. Nathan structures his chapters around major concepts: Fintech, Bitcoin, Blockchain technology, Central Bank Digital Currency, centralized and decentralized finance and the future of global financial system. He notes the intellectual development of the odyssey of money in which Bretton Woods created a distinctive fiat money among global financial system.

Eric Hayes, Blockchain Architect

CHAPTER 1

ODYSSEY/ADVENTUROUS JOURNEY OF MONEY

The Odyssey / adventurous journey of MONEY is a captivating field of inquiry. The evolution of how humans exchange value and facilitate trade-from bartering to commodity money to metallic money to paper money to current electronic money / digital money / currency. The current digital / virtual currencies stored and transferred electronically via digital space. Virtual currency is a digital currency that is largely unregulated, issued and usually controlled by its developers, and used and accepted electronically among members of a specific virtual community. This form of electronic / virtual money has the benefit of being fast, secure, traceable, and accessible.

In essence, the history of money is the development over time of systems for the exchange, storage, and measurement of wealth. The concept of MONEY has taken many different forms in human evolutionary history. We as humans worked with the barter system – trading goods such as livestock, seashells, silk, spices, in exchange for land, food, materials such as metals. Throughout human history what people consider valuable has changed considerably. In essence, throughout human history, the concept of MONEY has taken different forms from trading goods, and services to coins, bills [bank notes], checks, credit cards / debit cards and DIGITAL WALLETS for VIRTUAL MONEY/currency.

When it comes to livestock, the first form of currency, and public frequently trade them for goods, and seashells which were found in Pacific and Indian oceans were traded as money. Then small pieces of metal as coins appeared- eventually bills [bank notes] represented the value of coins. The exchange of bills [bank notes] and coins transitioned to electronic transacting in the 1990's.

FIRST LET US LOOK AT THE HISTORY OF 'FIAT CURRENCY' AND HOW IT'S EVOLVED:

The outcome of the Bretton Woods meeting with delegates from forty-four countries on 1st of July 1944 was an 'International Gold Standard Agreement' where U.S Dollar was downgraded to gold at $35 per troy ounce and other currencies were disrated to the dollar and could be redeemed for gold at the U.S Treasury. The IMF was established, as was the international bank for Reconstruction and Development (IBRD) which would eventually become part of the World Bank. During that time, ordinary Americans were still banned from owning non-jewelry gold.

Prior to 1944, in the year 1931 Britain, most of the Commonwealth countries with the Bretton Woods marked a return to the gold standard. However, the Bretton Woods Agreement didn't work very well. Countries frequently devalued their currencies with respect to the U.S dollar and gold. In the year 1949, Britain devalued their Pound by about 30% from $4.30 to $2.80, and many other countries followed Britain. By 1971, the Bretton Woods Agreement broke down after the U.S stopped honoring the convertibility of U.S dollars to gold. Then there was a big drop in U.S gold reserves and an increase in foreign claims on U.S dollars.

HOW 'FIAT CURRENCIES' COME INTO EXISTENCE IN FINANCIAL SYSTEM:

Quantitative Easing known as QE often comes up in fiat currencies. So, public describe this as 'printing money.' QE is a metaphor for an authority, generally a CENTRAL BANK – increasing the amount of money in circulation in order to stimulate a flagging economy. So, public worry that this additional money dilutes the value of existing money, and this makes public worry about the sustainability of the 'Fiat system.' In brief, Quantitative Easing is a form of monetary policy in which a central bank (like the U.S Federal Reserve) purchases predetermined amounts of government bonds or other financial assets in order to stimulate economic activity. In essence, Quantitative Easing is a form of monetary policy used by central bank to increase the domestic money supply and spur economic activity. Quantitative Easing creates new bank reserves, providing banks with more liquidity and encouraging lending and investment.

Quantitative Easing is often implemented where interest rates hover near zero and economic growth is stalled. To execute QE central banks, buy government bonds and other securities, injecting bank reserves into the economy. Increasing the supply of money lowers interest rates further and provides liquidity to the banking system, allowing banks to lend with easier terms. However, as money is increased in an economy, the risk of inflation looms.

THE FLOWCHART OF BANKING SYSTEM

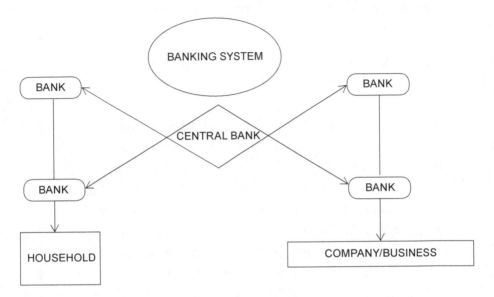

HOW DOES QUANTITATIVE EASING WORKS:

The CENTRAL BANK buys assets such as bonds, funds from the private commercial sector, commercial banks, asset managers, and hedge funds in the secondary market. The bonds that have already been issued and now traded by financial market participants.

Central banks form an image of the private sector as having a balance of two things – MONEY and NON-MONEY and other financial assets. Central banks control those balances by buying financial assets from the private sector to add money, or by selling financial assets to the private sector to remove money. But when it comes to bonds, they are generally safe assets. Their value is affected by interest rates – the central bank has some control over it. Central banks buy bonds from certain clearing banks. Central banks start the QE journey by buying government bonds – US Treasury etc.

The Schematic diagram portrays HOW SYSTEM OF
CENTRAL BANK WORKS

SYSTEM OF CENTRAL BANK

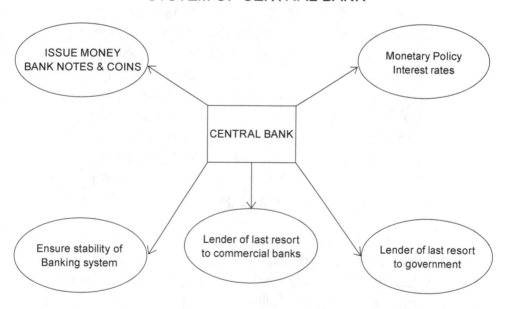

CHAPTER 2

FIAT CURRENCY AND FINANCIAL TECHNOLOGY (FINTECH)

Fiat currency is not backed by a physical commodity such as gold or silver, but instead backed by the government that issued it. Fiat currency derives its value from the decisions of the central bank, rather than through reserves of assets. In brief, the value of fiat currency is derived from the relationship between supply and demand and the stability of the issuing government, rather than the worth of a commodity backing it. In essence, fiat money generally does not have intrinsic value and does not have use value. It has value only because the individuals who use it as a unit of accounting or in the case of currency, a medium of exchange.

Financial technology or Fintech is a term referring to the integration of technology into offerings by financial services companies in order to improve their use and delivery service. For example, Artificial Intelligence (AI), blockchain, cloud computing, and big data etc. are considered the key areas of Fintech. In industry, Fintech has been used to automate investments, insurance, trading, banking services and risk management. Fintech can apply to any innovation into how people transact businesses, from the invention of digital money to double-entry bookkeeping. The crucial aspect of the use of artificial intelligence tools to automate the application, screening, and approval processes involved in the provision of credit, insurance, and other financial products. These factors reduce the costs of entry for new companies / businesses and products in addition to erasing some of the advantages of established companies / businesses such as experienced employees, expertise, deep pockets, and name recognition. Advanced technologies help overcome one of the major barriers to rapid change from the user perspective - network effects, which in this context refers to the convenience of adopting a payment method or service that is already in widespread use, rather than switching to a new alternative. Another Fintech innovation is the advent of mobile / smartphone-based applications designed to facilitate the use of money and banking.

Artificial Intelligence (AI) algorithms can furnish insight into customer spending habits, allowing financial institutions to better understand their clients. Chatbots are Artificial Intelligence (AI) driven tools that banks are starting to utilize to help with customer service. Big data can predict client investments and market changes in order to create new strategies and portfolios, analyze customer spending habits, improve fraud detection, and create marketing strategies. The decentralized nature of blockchain can eliminate the need for a third party to execute transactions. Fintech also includes the development and use of cryptocurrencies such as Bitcoin.

In essence, Fintech is utilized to help companies, business owners, and consumers better manage their financial operations, processes, and lives. Fintech is composed of specialized software and algorithms that are used on computers and smartphones. Examples of Fintech applications include payment apps, peer-to-peer lending apps, investments apps, crypto apps etc.

SOME OF THE MOST ACTIVE AREAS OF FINTECH INNOVATION INCLUDE THE FOLLOWING:

*Cryptocurrency – BITCOIN, ETHEREUM, DIGITAL TOKENS (non-fungible-tokens) and digital cash. These rely upon blockchain technology, which is distributed ledger technology (DLT) that maintains records on a network of computers (nodes) but has no center ledger. Blockchain allows for SMART CONTRACTS which utilize code to automatically execute contracts between parties such as buyers and sellers.

* Open banking

* Simplify and streamline the insurance industry

* Help financial services firms meet industry compliance rules.

* Utilize algorithms to automate investment advice to lower its cost and increase accessibility.

* Underbanked services that seek to serve disadvantaged or low-income individuals.

* Cybersecurity

* Artificial Intelligence (AI) Chatbots.

The main question is: Will 'Fiat money' survive in the years to come?

Some believe that public as a whole have some challenges in the GLOBAL DIGITAL ECONOMY in the form of DIGITAL CURRENCY – 'CRYPTOCURRENCIES.'

LET US SEE THE DIFFERENCE BETWEEN 'FIAT CURRENCY' AND 'VIRTUAL CURRENCY':

Fiat Currency is money that is issued by decree of a government. The value of a fiat currency is based on the strength of the issuing country's economy. For instance, the Dollar is considered one of the global economy's most valuable currencies since United States of America is one of the world's largest and strongest economies. The idea of value as it relates to currency shifted again in the twenty-first century with the rise of DIGITAL CURRENCIES such as BITCOIN and others. In essence, hard currency rarely needs to change hands, and the reliance on digital transactions has helped to give rise to a new way to pay: CRYPTOCURRENCY. The first such form, BITCOIN, replaced the CENTRAL AUTHORITY of a bank with peer-to-peer COMPUTER TECHNOLOGY. Today, we see tremendous growth in several cryptocurrencies. BITCOIN is like a digital ledger book. In other words, the computer code upon which it is based keeps everyone honest by making account balances and transactions public. The identities of the people who use BITCOIN, on the other hand, remain hidden.

CHAPTER 3

WHAT IS CRYPTOCURRENCY?

A CRYPTOCURRENCY is a digital currency designed to work as medium of exchange via a computer network that is not reliant on any central authority, such as a government or bank, to uphold or maintain it. CRYPTOCURRENCY is a centralized system for verifying that the parties to a transaction have the money they claim to have, eliminating the need for traditional intermediaries such as banks, when funds are being transferred between two entities.

Let us see what 'BITCOIN' is: It is the most prominent member of a NEW CLASS OF ELECTRONIC MONEY known as CRYPTOCURRENCY, which exists ONLY in the DIGITAL WORLD. Cryptocurrency has underlying digital technology in the block chain, which is a series of blocks that when combined, act as a permanent, unalterable ledger, detailing the HISTORY of transactions in a CRYPTOCURRENCY. Block chain plays an important role for investing cryptocurrency.

BITCOIN:

BITCOIN (BTC) runs on a blockchain a digital ledger logging transaction distributed across a network of numerous computers. The additions to the digital distributed legers have to be verified – by proof of work. Bitcoin is the most prominent member of the class of electronic money known as

CRYPTOCURRENCY, which exists only in the digital space. It is often compared to a DIGITAL LEDGER BOOK. The COMPUTER CODE upon which it is based keeps everyone honest by making account balances / transactions, all of which are electronic, are fully visible as public digital ledgers maintained on the Internet. However, a few cryptographic concepts are among the building BLOCKS/ records for bitcoin. These have to do with maintaining the confidentiality of transacting parties and the integrity of the public digital ledgers. Also, the identities of the people who use BITCOIN, on the other hand, remains hidden.

Let us look at the DIGITAL PUBLIC and PRIVATE KEYS involve in Bitcoin:

These are individual user 'IDENTITY.' The public digital keys are distributed widely without compromising security. One must know both the username and password to operate the account. These digital keys constitute the essential elements and anonymous digital payment systems.

Bitcoin is the very first digital asset of value that can be transferred over the Internet without any specific third party having to approve the transaction. It is an asset that is transferred from one individual owner to another individual than moving through a series of third party – debits or credits via one or more banks.

Bitcoins are digital assets or coins whose ownership is recorded on an electronic ledger that is updated simultaneously on several thousands of computers around the globe that connect and circulate with each other. This electronic ledger is known as bitcoin's BLOCKCHAIN. Transactions that record transfer of ownership of those coins are created and validated according to a protocol, a list of rules that define how things work and which therefore updates to the electronic ledger. The protocol is implemented by software application that participants run on their computers. The computers running the software applications are known as 'NODES' of the network [NODES- A Node is a computer that connects to cryptocurrency network]. Each NODE independently validated all pending transactions wherever they arise and updated its own record of the electronic ledger with validated BLOCKS / records of confirmed transactions. Specialist NODES called miners, bundle together valid transactions into BLOCKS / records and distribute those BLOCKS / records to NODES across the network. Any individual can purchase bitcoins, own them, and send them to others. However, every bitcoin transaction is recorded and shared publicly in plain text on bitcoin's blockchain.

Any individual can create bitcoins for themselves, and this is known as block creating process – 'MINING.' Much of the mining of bitcoin is carried out by specialized devices known as ASIC [Application Specific Integrated Circuits]. ASICs are built machines containing computer chips designed with a single, specific purpose.

BITCOIN and OTHERS:

Bitcoin is the first category of CRYPTOCURRENCY in the financial world. It is widely used and accepted around the world. Bitcoin does not involve encryption.

Bitcoin is a DECENTRALIZED DIGITAL CURRENCY that uses peer-to-peer technology and is referred to as

BLOCKCHAIN. This is to verify transactions. Bitcoin runs on HIGH-POWERED COMPUTER NETWORK that stores its code and BLOCKCHAIN, making it a secure system that is difficult for hackers to attack.

There are several thousands of cryptocurrencies in the global landscape. All categories of cryptocurrencies share certain characteristics. They are all forms of DIGITAL CURRENCY that allow for electronic transactions. However, there are some key differences among them.

LITECOIN: This is a decentralized digital currency that operates on an open-source global payment NOT controlled by a central authority such as a bank or government. It offers a faster transaction time than BITCOIN.

RIPPLE (XRP): It is a global payment network that serves major banks and financial institutions, including Bank of America and the Royal Bank of Canada. Ripple's main focus is as a payment settlement asset exchange and remittance system, similar to SWIFT system for international money and security transfers used by banks and financial intermediaries dealing across currencies.

SOLANA (SOL): Developed to help power decentralized finance (DeFi) uses, decentralized applications and smart contracts. It runs on unique hybrid proof-of-stake and proof-of-history mechanisms to process transactions quickly and securely. This is a solid competitor to Ethereum with faster transaction speeds and lower fees. This is a proof-stake blockchain. This is one of the most popular cryptocurrencies trading today. It is a decentralized and open source blockchain platform designed to be scalable, fast, and secure. It can process a significantly higher number of transactions than other popular blockchain platforms like Ethereum and bitcoin.

DOGECOIN (DOGE): It is a Bitcoin-based digital cryptocurrency. This is the most famous called 'meme coin.' There is no limit on the number of Dogecoins that can be created. It is a peer-to-peer, open-source cryptocurrency. Users can purchase and sell Dogecoin in digital currency exchange.

CHAINLINK: This is a cryptocurrency based on a decentralized oracle network, which allows it to connect data from the outside world to any blockchain. This structure gives developers more opportunities to build flexible, secure applications.

CARDANO (ADA): It works like Ethereum to enable 'smart contracts and decentralized applications. This is a blockchain which offers decentralized financial products, similar to Ethereum. But operates on a proof-of-stake blockchain. This lets people mine or validate block transactions according to how many coins they have. It is different from most blockchains. You create tokens on Cardano without smart contracts.

STELLAR (XLM): This open blockchain technology can be used by anyone but was primarily designed to support large transactions between financial institutions. In essence, it is an open-source, decentralized protocol for digital currency to fiat money low0cost transfers which allows cross-border transactions between any pair of currencies. The platform's source code is hosted on GitHub.

POLKAKOT: This is a proof-of-stake cryptocurrency designed to secure users' identities by connecting blockchains and networks. Polkadot's network is capable of interacting with other blockchain networks. It allows developers to create decentralized applications on its platform.

BINANCE (BNB): This cryptocurrency serves as a payment method for trading fees associated with the Binance Exchange where users can trade cryptocurrencies. One of the largest crypto exchanges. BNB can be used for trading, payment processing, booking travel arrangements. It can also be traded and exchanged for other forms of cryptocurrency – Ethereum or bitcoin.

COINBASE: It is a public traded company that operates a cryptocurrency exchange platform. Coinbase is a distributed company, all employees operate via remote work. It offers products for both retail and institutional cryptocurrency investors, as well as other related cryptocurrency products.

TETHER (USDT): Tether's value is connected to regular FIAT currencies to keep its price more stable than its competitors. In other words, it is backed by fiat currencies (U.S. dollars & the EU dollars). This type of arrangement is known as a stablecoin.

MONERO: It offers users more privacy than other cryptocurrencies. It uses a special technique called ring signatures which hide the identities of the sender and receiver of every transaction as well as the amount.

SHIBA INU (SHIB): This is another meme coin. This is an Ethereum-based altcoin other than bitcoin. This is the project's foundational currency.

DASH: This is an open-source cryptocurrency, which means it is collaboratively produced, freely shared and published transparently. It supports daily transactions and can be used as cash or credit or via PayPal.

ZCASH: It uses cryptography and coding to provide enhanced privacy to users. Users can choose whether or not to anonymize the information associated with their transactions.

WAVES: This is a blockchain designed to help users create and launch custom crypto tokens. The platform is designed to make it easier to develop new types of tokens without needing to understand the complicated programming language.

NEO: It is a blockchain-based platform that resembles Ethereum. It can process 10,000 transactions per second.

NANO: It is much more environmentally friendly. It does not charge transaction fees.

LISK: This is an opensource blockchain application platform. The utility token affiliated with Lisk is LSK, which can be used to pay for transaction fees on the Lisk blockchain.

TRON (TRX): This is a blockchain-based decentralized platform. It aims to eliminate the middleman between content creators and content consumers by allowing consumers to directly pay creators to access their content. This is a blockchain designed to run smart contracts and other Defi applications.

UNISWAP: This is a decentralized exchange that runs on the Ethereum blockchain. It allows trades in other cryptocurrencies, and offers its own native tokens, which give holders rights to change the protocols governing the exchange.

STABLE COIN: Stable coin is a cryptocurrency that aims to maintain price stability by pegging its monetary value to a given fiat currency, typically on a one-to-one basis. Stable coins offer a less risky alternative to store money on the blockchain and facilitate payments between individuals and institutions alike. They are accessible worldwide to anyone with an Internet connection and are functional 24/7. They are fast and inexpensive to use. Through the use of SMART CONTRACTS, transactions can be automatically executed within specific parameters. It can be used for trading, borrowing and lending, earning yield, as an alternative to banking for sending remittances, as stores of value etc.

Examples of Fiat-based STABLE COINS:

* **USDC [Coinbase]**

* **TETHER**

* **GUSD [Gemini]**

* **BUSD [Binance]**

BITCOIN AND MINING:

Bitcoin mining is a complex computational and technological process of validating the bitcoin transactions over the bitcoin network. It is like a process of validating a block/record on the chain network and getting paid in bitcoins. Mining is the process of adding transactions records to bitcoins' public ledger of past transactions.

There are many ways to earn bitcoins. Mining for bitcoins is how bitcoin by participating in the network. Anyone gets started earning BITCOINS. Mining for Bitcoins is usually handled by special mining hardware. This mining hardware is expensive as well as specialized. It also needs BITCOIN MINING SOFTARE to connect to the blockchain and the mining pool. The mining pool is a collection of many miners jointly working together and then splitting the rewards of their efforts.

Let us see the different mining Bitcoin software:

*   CGminer. It is open source and is available for Windows, Linux, and OS. www.github.com/ckolivas/cgminer

*   Bitcoin-QT. https://bitcoin.org/en/download.

*   Multiminerapp: Download it at www.multiminerapp.com

WHAT IS 'DIGITAL WALLET'?

In terms of VIRTUAL MONEY/currency, digital transactions are stored. It can be a piece of paper, a hardware device that plugs into your computer or an app on your computer or even in your mobile device. These DIGITAL WALLETS allow users to send and receive DIGITAL CURRENCY, by providing an INTERNET ADDRESS to which tokens can be sent. In other words, DIGITAL WALLET is method of storing the public and private keys needed to access your DIGITAL CURRENCY.

Let us see how to maintain a DIGITAL WALLET:

A digital currency needs a DIGITAL WALLET. Crypto wallets hold public and private encryption keys. These keys wallets are used for buying or selling digital currency. There are two categories of digital wallets:

*A hot wallet is connected to the Internet. Any app-based wallet or a wallet that access via computer's browser is known as hot wallet These hot wallets make accessing crypto easier.

*A cold wallet is not directly connected to the Internet. These are small portable devices similar to USB drives.

Anyone can purchase a CRYPTOCURRENCY:

* **Before you purchase your first cryptocurrency coin, you will have to have a place to keep it in Cryptocurrency WALLETS. Most exchanges offer a default wallet that you can use. However, you can have a secure wallet known as a cold wallet.**

* **Try to select an exchange or trading platform.**

* **Once you have selected an exchange, create an account and verify your identity – personal information, copy of your driver's license and proof of your address.**

* **You must make a decision on how much you want to invest.**

*   **Once you have selected an exchange, set up an account and decided how much you want to spend, you are ready to make your purchase.**

But if you don't want to go through an exchange, or you want to convert cash to coins, another option is Bitcoin ATM. Insert cash, and the ATM will give you a QR CODE you can use to send the coins directly to your digital-WALLET.

Let us look at cryptocurrency exchange platforms:

Cryptocurrency exchanges are online platforms that enable users to BUY, SELL and TRADE various cryptocurrencies. Many of these exchange platforms allow anyone to purchase cryptocurrencies with U.S dollars. From there, anyone can trade one type of cryptocurrency coin for another.

There are two types of cryptocurrency exchange platforms namely, CENTRALIZED and DECENTRALIZED.

Centralized exchange platforms are simple to use. Here transactions are facilitated through a third party. For example, Binance or Coinbase. To use a centralized exchange platform, he or she first registers and proof of identification, this grant-access to certain privileges that decentralized exchange platform does not offer.

Decentralized exchange platforms have a steeper learning curve. Transactions on a decentralized exchange platforms are made directly between traders. For example, on the decentralized platforms trades are conducted across user-owned distributed ledgers. This makes the system much more difficult to hack.

When it comes to 'public key', it is similar to username – sharable string numbers and letters that allow users to send and receive DIGITAL CURRENCY. 'Private key' is like a password, a private number that allows an owner to access their DIGITAL CURRENCY.

Let's look at the advantages and disadvantages of cryptocurrency in global scale:

Advantages:

*   Cryptocurrency can directly impact and change important financial in global trade which can be made faster and more affordable through cryptocurrency TRANSACTIONS.

*   Cryptocurrency also can make global transfers more effectively and efficiently feeless, whilst online banking has struggled to keep these fees under one percent.

*   Blockchain TRANSACTIONS are the fastest type of financial transfer and are also one of the most SECURE due to every transaction being recorded.

*   Utilizing blockchain technology for transfers, as everything remains anonymous. Everyone can see the TRANSACTIONS happening and access the records at any time, but identities remain unknown. In essence, it furnishes a sense of privacy and security that many have longed for with their TRANSACTIONS.

* There are numerous advantages to having CRYPTOCURENCY. In other words, the developers / designers of network of Bitcoin systems, they have built properties into their systems that have made cryptocurrency a competitive alternative FINANCIAL SYSTEMS, for example, Electronic Payment Systems such as PayPal, credit cards, banks.

* They have LOW transaction costs unlike other systems such as Electronic Payment Systems – PayPal where transfer of money with banks tends to have expensive fees. In essence, it costs less to transfer money from one individual to another individual. Businesses also don't have to account for added expenses which eventually translate into lower prices for the consumers / customers. Moreover, immigrants who left their home country to find work and want to send remittances back to their families.

* In the twenty-first century, banks and financial institutions around the globe don't serve poor, rural areas, particularly smaller countries. However, CRYPTOCURRENCY works to combat poverty and oppression around the world. In other words, FREE and OPEN access to basic financial services could easily help those who are impoverished and oppressed. Bitcoin furnishes any individual with Internet access with robust financial services.

* Cryptocurrency has its speed, its facilitation of digital nature of micro-payments and its low transaction costs. This leads to innovating new marketing and

business models, financial opportunities and online business strategies.

* Cryptocurrency is also untaxable as no central body owns it. In brief, People are in control of finances of cryptocurrency, which means further savings for businesses and companies. This can deeply benefit larger businesses, which means funds can be spent on improving the businesses or extending growth instead of paying higher business taxes.

* Developers / designers of open source of CRYPTOCURRENCY can extend functionalities by writing API's and writing application specific code to interact with networks of CRYPTOCURRENCY.

* Transactions of CRYPTOCURRENCY process quicker than checks and transfer of bank facilitated money transfers. These transactions are recorded in CRYPTOCURRENCY's public ledger. In other words, the transactions are recorded in the permanent transaction BLOCKCHAIN.

* 'The PRIVATE KEY' [cryptographic PASSWORD] is the only way money can be accessed. In essence, no bank, company, or central government can FREEZE your ASSETS.

Disadvantages:

* CRYPTOCURRENCY fluctuates in value.

* There are digital security breaches.

*   There are open opportunities in Bitcoin for criminals to partake in illegal activities such as money laundering, funding for terrorists, and the exchange of illegal goods and services.

USE OF CRYPTOCURRENCY FOR CONSUMERS / CUSTOMERS AROUND THE GLOBE:

One of objectives of cryptocurrency is to expand access to financial service tools to many people who are barred from entering the traditional banking system. It encourages self-sovereignty, the ability for individuals to maintain control over their data, be it identity information or their money. As cryptocurrencies gain more popularity, more and more companies are accepting them as a form of payment.

There are several companies such as **MICROSOFT, T-MOBILE, PAYPAL, STARBUCKS, HOME DEPOT, EXPEDIA, WHOLE FOODS, SUBWAY, PIZZA HUT etc**. accept cryptocurrency as payment or use it for transactions. They partner with payment processors such as GoCoin, Coinbase, and BitPay to accept cryptocurrencies – Bitcoin, Ethereum, Dogecoin, Cardano etc. Around 50% of companies around the world accept cryptocurrencies as a form of payment. 90% of retailers accept cryptocurrency as a form of payment.

CHAPTER 4

BLOCKCHAIN

In a layman's term, a blockchain is an encrypted network used to store, distribute and generate information. The key to a blockchain lies in the way it connects the information on it. In other words, a blockchain like a DATABASE that runs on a network of computers. A series of BLOCKS / records that, when combined, act as a permanent, unalterable LEDGER, detailing the history of TRANSACTIONS in CRYPTOCURRENCY. It is a DATABASE shared across many different computers. In brief, the blockchain started life as a DISTRIBUTED LEDGER used to authenticate a CRYPTOCURRENCY's transaction history. Now, it is being used as the basis for all sorts of secure transactions, from secure information exchange to smart contracts, art ownership and more.

Before going further, it is vital to note that not every blockchain is made the same. While there are a number of variable features, two of the most important are the OPENESS of the platform (Public or private) and the level of permissions required to add information to the blockchain (permissioned or permissionless). Public blockchains (like Bitcoin) are open for anyone to read and view, while private blockchains can only be viewed by a chosen group of people. Similarly, permissioned blockchains permit just a select group of users to write / generate transactions for the ledger to record and commit very few new blocks for addition to the chain. In contrast, permissionless blockchains allow anyone to contribute and add data to the ledger.

In brief, A blockchain is a shared ledger of transactions between parties in a network, not controlled by a single central authority. You can think of a ledger like a record book. It records and stores all transactions between users in chronological order. Instead of one authority controlling this ledger (like a bank), an identical copy of the ledger is held by all users on the network, called NODES (computers).

In a blockchain, consecutive, time-stamped transactions are grouped into segments known as BLOCKS/records. Each BLOCK / record is sealed with complex encryption. The next BLOCK / record links to the previous BOCK / record, and the chain grows, single BLOCK by single BLOCK / record, as more TRANSACTIONS occur. All the BLOCKS / records on a blockchain are related to one another. Each BLOCK / record is protected with complex encryption. As BLOCKS / records get linked, they create a permanent TRANSACTION history visible to the entire network. Since they are also decentralized, there is no intermediary overseeing the transaction database.

No single user can override or alter the blockchain's history. That makes blockchain an extremely secure system. Blockchains are an excellent tool for launching a whole new era of FINANCIAL INNOVATION. They eliminate the need for centralized authority to oversee TRANSACTIONS, blockchains have the potential to disrupt many parts of the FINANCIAL SERVICES industry, including banks, brokers and lenders. Furthermore, blockchain technology can be useful for providing banking type services to people who have historically avoided doing business with banking institutions.

The blockchain requires the participation of many different users dedicating computing power to growing and maintaining the blockchain. A blockchain incentivizes this participation by rewarding those users who grow the blockchain with native CRYPTOCURRENCY, a process known as MINING.

The flowchart illustrates HOW BLOCKCHAIN WORKS

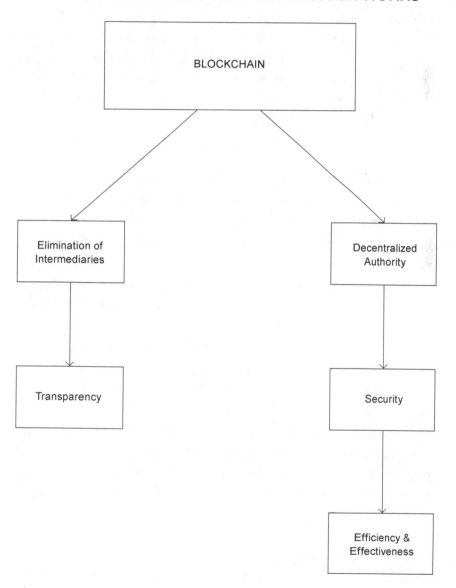

BLOCKCHAIN:

A Blockchain is a 'DISTRIBUTED LEDGER' with a growing list of BLOCKS / records that are securely linked together through CRYPTOGRAPHIC HASHES. For the purposes of a cryptocurrency, a HASH serves as a digital fingerprint of a transaction. Each transaction has a unique HASH. Only that specific transaction with all the relevant information coded in exactly the same fashion as before, will reproduce that HASH. The HASH function used in the bitcoin protocol is known as SHA-256 (SHA stands for Secure Hash Algorithm). A cryptographic algorithm with 256 bits of security is seen as highly secure.

A HASH is like a digital fingerprint; it is unique to each piece of data on the blockchain. Users put information regarding their transaction {name of receiver and sender along with the amount transferred) into cryptographic HASHING algorithm - a complex mathematical formula – and receive asset of letters and numbers that is distinct to that transaction. The specific input, if unchanged, will always produce the same exact HASH. If, however, any part of the data is changed (for example, a malicious actor changes the amount transferred), the HASH would change to an entirely different set of characters and make it incompatible with the rest of the chain. Therefore, even without seeing the details of the transaction, nodes (computers) can quickly tell that the data within the block has been tampered with and reject that version of the ledger. It is this cryptographic security that makes blockchain ledgers more trustworthy and almost immutable. Example of HASH: Input HASH output (using SHA 256 algorithm).

Each BLOCK / record contains CRYPTOGRAHIC HASH of the previous BLOCK / record, a timestamp, and transaction data

[Merkle tree where data nodes are represented by leaves]. The Merkle root guarantees the data integrity of the set of transactions tampering with anyone of them changes its HASH, which in turn changes all the HASHES on that branch of the Merkle tree, all the way up to and including the root HASH.

Since each BLOCK / record contains information about the previous BLOCK / record, they effectively form a CHAIN with (compare linked data structure), with each additional BLOCK / record linking to the ones before it. BLOCKCHAIN transactions are irreversible in that, once they are recorded, the data in any given BOLCK / record cannot be altered retroactively without altering all subsequent BLOCKS / records. Blockchains Are managed by a per-to-peer computer network for use as a public distributed ledger, where nodes [a computer or other device that helps maintain a cryptocurrency's BLOCKCHAIN'S by participating in the transaction] collectively adhere to consensus algorithm protocol to add and validate new transaction BLOCKS /records.

In essence, blockchains are important because they allow for new efficiency and reliability in the exchange of valuable and private information that once required a third party to facilitate, such as the movement of money and the validation of identity. Blockchains are powerful tools because they create honest systems that self-correct without the need of a third party to enforce the rules. Blockchains accomplish the enforcement of rules through their consensus algorithm. The consensus is the process of developing an agreement among a group of commonly mistrusting shareholders. These are the full nodes on the network. The full nodes are validating transactions that are entered into the network to be recorded as part of the distributed ledger.

BLOCKCHAIN STRUCTURE / DESIGN:

A BLOCKCHAIN is a decentralized, distributed, and often public, DIGITAL LEDGE consisting of BLOCKS / records that used to record transactions across numerous computers so that any involved BLOCK / record CANNOT be altered retroactively, without the alteration of all subsequent BLOCKS / records. This allows the participants to VERIFY and AUDIT transactions independently and relatively inexpensively. Its features can increase the transparency and traceability of data and financial assets, facilitate access and improve the efficiency of transactions. In brief, blockchain utilizes distributed ledger technology (DLT) to store information verified by cryptography among a group of users, which agreed through a pre -defined network protocols, often without the control of a central authority. The marriage of these technologies gives blockchain networks key characteristics that can remove the need for trust, and therefore enable a secure transfer of value and data directly between parties. Due to this unique ability, blockchain technology can diminish the role of intermediaries, who can command power, collect significant fees, slow economic activity, and are not necessarily trustworthy or altruistic keepers of personal information.

A blockchain database is managed autonomously using a per-to-peer network and distributed timestamping server. A blockchain has been known as a value-exchange protocol. A blockchain can maintain title rights because, when properly set up to detail the exchange agreement, it provides a record that compels offer and acceptance. In essence, a blockchain can be seen as consisting of several layers namely, infrastructure, networking [node discovery, information propagation & verification], consensus [proof of work & proof of stake], data [blocks / records, transactions], application [smart contracts / decentralized applications]

When it comes to BLOCKS / records Block / record holds batches of valid transactions that are hashed and encoded into a Merkle tree. Each BLOCK / record includes the cryptographic hash of the prior BLOCK / record in the blockchain, linking the two. The linked BLOCKS / records for a chain. Block time / record time is the average time it takes for the network to generate one extra BLOCK / record in the blockchain. By the time of BLOCK / record completion, the included data becomes verifiable.

BLOCKCHAIN AND CRYPTOCURRENCY:

A blockchain is a data structure that makes it possible to create a DIGITAL LEDGER of data and share it among a network. We find there are three different categories of blockchains namely,

*   Public blockchains. For example, BITCOIN which are large, distributed networks that are run through a CRYPTOCURRENCY which is a UNIQUE bit of data that can be traded between two parties. These Public blockchains are open for anyone to participate at any level and usually have open-source code.

*   Private blockchains. These are known as DISTRIBUTED LEDGER TECHNOLOGY [in short, DLT] They DO NOT use a token / cryptocurrency. These tend to be smaller and do not utilize a token or cryptocurrency. The membership of these Private blockchains is closely controlled and are favored by

consortiums that have trusted members and trade confidential information.

* Permissioned blockchains. For example, RIPPLE is where individuals can play within the network and are large distributed systems that use a native token.

The above categories of blockchains are contributing to what is known as Web3 [Web 3.0]. Blockchains create permanent records and histories of TRANSACTIONS. However, these records are NOT permanent records for that matter. When data is recorded in a blockchain, it is difficult to change or remove it. However, when someone wants to add a record to a blockchain, users int eh network who have validation control verify the proposed transaction of the record.

The Schematic diagram illustrates the main categories of BLOCKCHAIN

The main categories of BLOCKCHAIN segmented by permission model

			READ	WRITE	COMMIT	EXAMPLE
BLOCKCHAIN TYPES	OPEN	Public Permissionless	Open to anyone	Anyone	Anyone	Bitcoin, Ethereum
		Public Permissioned	Open to anyone	Authorised participants	All or subset of authorised participants	Supply chain ledger for retail brand viewable by public
	CLOSED	Consortium	Restricted to an authorized set of participants	Authorised participants	All or subset of authorised participants	Multiple banks operating a shared ledger
		Private permissioned "enterprise'	Fully private or restricted to a limited set of authorized nodes	Network operator only	Network operator only	External bank ledger shared between parent company and subsidiaries

Public blockchains are open for anyone to read and view.

Private blockchains can only be viewed by a chosen group of people.

Permissioned blockchains permit just a select group of users to write [that is: generate transactions for the LEDGER to record] and commit [that is: verify new blocks for addition to the chain].

In contrast, **permissionless blockchains** allow anyone to contribute and add data to the LEDGER.

STRUCTURE OF BLOCKCHAIN:

Each blockchain is STRUCTURED differently. The way that bitcoin coordinates the organization and input of new data comprises three core ELEMENTS namely:

* **BLOCK,**

* **CHAIN and**

* **NETWORK.**

Block/record: A list of transactions recorded into a ledger over a given period – the size, period and triggering event for blocks / records is different for every blockchain.

Chain: A hash that links one block to another, mathematically chaining them together.

Network: The network is composed of full nodes (computers). Each node contains a complete record of all the transactions that were ever recorded in that blockchain. The nodes are located all over the globe and can be operated by anyone.

The hash in blockchain is created from the data that was in the previous block/record. The hash is a fingerprint of this data and locks blocks/records in order and time.

The BLOCKCHAIN structure and the
FLOWCHART HOW IT WORKS

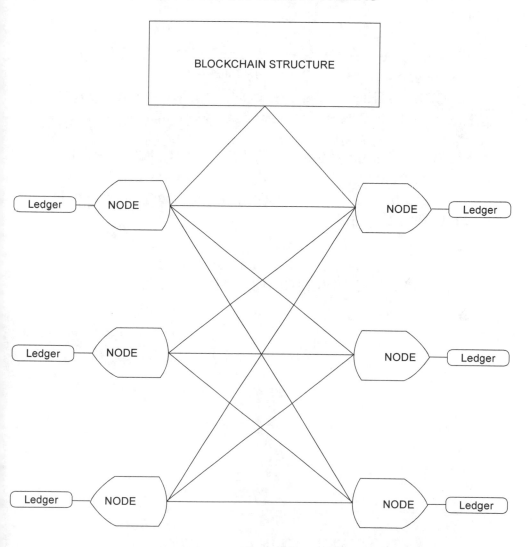

Network: The network is composed of FULL NODES. Each node contains a complete record of all the transactions that were ever recorded in that blockchain. Nodes (computers) running an algorithm that is securing the network. Each node (computer) contains a complete record of all the transactions that were ever recorded in the blockchain. The nodes (computers) are located globally and can be operated by any individual.

In essence, the BLOCKCHAIN is a PUBLIC LEDGER of all transactions in the BITCOIN NETWORK, and the NODES are COMPUTERS that are recording entries into that ledger. However, BITCOIN is the rules that govern this system.

NODES safeguard the NETWORK by MINING for the cryptocurrency BITCOIN. New BITCOINS are created as a reward for processing transactions and recording them inside the BLOCKCHAIN.

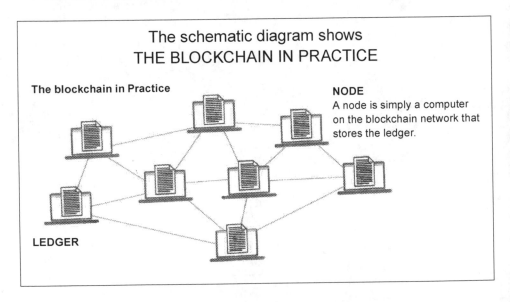

The schematic diagram shows
THE BLOCKCHAIN IN PRACTICE

The blockchain in Practice

NODE
A node is simply a computer on the blockchain network that stores the ledger.

LEDGER

BLOCKCHAIN IN PRACTICE

A blockchain is shared LEDGER of transactions among parties in a NETWORK (Nodes/Computers), NOT controlled by a single central authority. A LEDGER is like a record book- it records and stores all transactions among users in chronological order. An identical copy of the LEDGER is held by all users on the NETWORK known as NODES (COMPUTERS).

LEDGER:A ledger is a list of all transactions made on the blockchain. It is made up of a chain of BLOCKS/records.

DISTRIBUTED: All copies of one document are spread among users. They are constantly and automatically synchronized, hence identical at all times.

COMPARISON OF BITCOIN AND BLOCKCHAIN:

The term BITCOIN and BLOCKCHAIN are often used interchangeably, but they are NOT the same. BITCOIN has a BLOCKCHAIN. The Bitcoin blockchain is the underlying protocol that enables the secure transfers of BITCOIN. The BITCOIN is the name of the CRYPTOCURRENCY that powers the bitcoin network.

The BLOCKCHAIN is a class of software, and BITCOIN is a specific CRYPTOCURRENCY. BLOCKCHAIN originated with the creation of BITCOIN. BITCOINS are powerful tools. Each BLOCKCHAIN has its own algorithms for creating agreement within its network on the entries being added.

There are several thousands of blockchains and blockchains-based applications globally in use. These systems allow for the creation of NFT [Nonfungible Token]- the use of cryptocurrency in gaming, faster movement of money through distributed network, and the development of secure trustworthy applications and hardware.

ICO [Initial Coin Offerings] is another blockchain innovation. They are a type of 'SMART CONTRACT' that allows the issuer to offer a token in exchange for investment funds.

Let us see what SMART CONTRACT is:

SMART CONTRACT is a self-executing computer program. This performs pre-defined tasks based upon to predetermined set of criteria / conditions. These cannot be altered once deployed, their integrity is protected by the public and transparent nature of blockchain.

Smart contracts can include deadlines that make them useful for time-sensitive transactions and also reduce counter party risk.

Atomicity &Smart contract: Smart contracts are usually set up such that the entire transaction will fail if any of the multiple steps involved in it cannot be executed.

Smart contracts can facilitate financial transactions. Smart contracts could also be used for commercial transactions.

CHAPTER 5

BLOCKCHAIN TECHNOLOGY

The blockchain is a public electronic ledger of all transactions in the bitcoin network, and the nodes are computers that are recording entries into that ledger. The bitcoin protocol is the rules that govern this system. In brief, blockchain technologies are the RULES and standards for how an ELECTRONIC LEDGER is created and maintained. For example, BITCOIN, ETHEREUM, NXT.

Blockchain technology contain the following concepts:

* **A data store and or database that records changes in the data, the most known are financial transactions.**

* **Replication of the data store across several systems in real time.**

* **Peer to peer network**

* **Digital signatures to provide ownership and authenticity and hashes for references.**

The public ledger is known as BLOCKCHAIN since, once the transactions coming onto the network are grouped into BLOCKS / records of data and validated, the BLOCKS/ records are their chained together, Each BLOCK / record includes a HASH of preceding BLOCK / record, thereby linking them to one another. Thus, each new BLOCK / record is recurrently linked to all of the preceding BLOCKS / records on the chain.

Advantages of Blockchain Technology:

Blockchain has enhanced DIGITAL LEDGER TECHNOLOGY into a truly decentralized format that eliminates the need for a trusted intermediary to process and validate transactions between two parties. The transactions ledger cannot be overridden, hacked or manipulated.

Blockchain technology in a nutshell:

Blockchain technology is being used as the basis for all types of secure transactions from secure information exchange to smart contracts and more. At its simplest, a blockchain is an encrypted network used to store, distribute and generate information. The basic storage unit for information on the blockchain is a set of transactions known as a BLOCK. All the BLOCKS on a blockchain are related to one another. Changing information on a given BLOCK would break the chain- and every computer [node] on the network would know about it. Each BLOCK is protected with complex encryption. As BLOCKS get linked, they create a permanent transaction history visible to the entire network. Since they are decentralized, there is no intermediary overseeing the transaction database. No single user can override or alter the blockchain's history. That makes it an extremely secure system.

Ethereum:

Ethereum has a public blockchain running on several thousand computers and the token on the blockchain is known as

'ETHER.' Ethereum is a bunch of 'protocols' written out as 'CODES' which is run as Ethereum software which creates Ethereum transactions containing data about Ether coins [ETH] recorded on Ethereum blockchain.

The main Ethereum network is a public, permissionless network where any individual can download and write software to connect to the network and start creating transactions and smart contracts, validate them, and mining BLOCKS / records without needing to sign up with any others.

It is an open-source crowdfunded project that built the Ethereum blockchains. Ethereum network allows anyone to create smart contracts, create decentralized organizations, and deploy decentralized applications.

Decentralized applications (dAPP) can manage digital assets and decentralized autonomous organizations (DAO). DAOs are a type of Ethereum application that represents a virtual entity within Ethereum. When you create a DAO, you can invite others to participate in the governance of the organization.

DAO membership structure:

Token-based membership, Share-based membership, and Reputation-based membership.

This is the second largest digital currency after Bitcoin. Ethereum is a decentralized software platform that enabled the development of contracts and decentralized apps.

How Decentralized Autonomous Organizations [DAO] work:

   * A group of people writes a SMART CONTRACT to govern the organization.

   * People add funds to the DAO and are given tokens that represent ownership.

[This structure works like stock in a company, But the members have control of the funds from day one.

   * When the funds have been raised, the DAO begins to operate by having members propose how to spend the money. Voting may be affected by how much ETHER the member risks or stakes in the DAO.

   * The members vote on these proposals.

   * When the predetermined time has passed and the predetermined number of votes has accrued, the proposal passes or fails.

   * Individuals act as contractors to service the DAO.

Let us see how the ETHEREUM NETWORK work:

To participate in the Ethereum network, Ethereum client software has to be utilized. Ethereum client software can be used to connect to the Ethereum network, validate transactions and BLOCKS/ records, create new transactions, create smart contracts, run smart contracts [as a matter of fact, Ethereum smart contracts are SHORT PROGRAMS that are stored on Ethereum's blockchain, replicated across all the nodes and are available for any individual to inspect] and mine for new BLOCKS / records. Then the computer becomes a NODE on the network, running an ETHEREUM VIRTUAL MACHINE [EVM] and becomes equivalent to all other nodes. EVM processes all the Ethereum transactions and BLOCKS / records and keeps track of all the account balances and results of the smart contracts. Each node on the Ethereum network runs the same EVM and processes the same data, resulting in them all having the same view. In essence, Ethereum client software will connect over the Internet to other people's computers running similar client software and start downloading the Ethereum blockchain from them to catch up with the latest state of the blockchain. It will validate that each BLOCKS / records conforms to the Ethereum protocol rules.

Ethereum token is known as 'ETHER' [ETH]. This cryptocurrency can be traded for other currencies like bitcoin.

Let us see the Ethereum blockchain ecosystem:

To set up Ethereum wallet-

* Go to www. Ethreum.org

* Click the download button.

* Open the Ethereum wallet.

* Choose Develop from the drop-down menu.

* Select one of the tests networks.

* Create a strong password.

* Click through the startup menu.

* Choose Develop -> Start Mining

DAO [Decentralized Autonomous Organization]. These are a type of Ethereum application that represents a virtual entity within Ethereum.

To build DAO:

* **Go to <u>www.ethereum.org/dao</u>**

* **Scroll down the page to the Code box and copy the code.**

* **Open the Ethereum wallet.**

* **Develop your DAO in the Ethereum wallet.**

CHAPTER 6

DIGITAL LEDGER TECHNOLOGY [DLT]

Digital Ledger Technology takes the form of electronic DATABASE that are maintained simultaneously and synchronized across a numerous of NODES [computers] on a network. The network, which is composed of many NODES, has no central point of authority. Information on each transaction is sent to every NODE on the network to be validated and grouped into timestamped BLOCKS / records of transactions. Each NODE maintains a copy of all transactions on the network. The transparency and decentralized nature of DIGITAL LEDGER TECHNOLOGY are essential elements of the technology's security. The transparency and decentralized nature of the DIGITAL LEDGER TECHNOLOGY would help ensure the integrity of transactions since any tampering by dishonest person would be easily detected. In essence, DLT is a technological infrastructure and protocols that allow simultaneous access, validation, and record updating across a networked database. It is the technology blockchains are created from, and the infrastructure allows users to view any changes and who made them, reduces the need to audit data, ensures data is reliable, and only provides access to those that need it.

Distributed ledgers are maintained by a network of nodes, each of which has a copy of the ledger, validates the information, and helps reach a consensus about its accuracy, all blockchains are distributed ledgers, but not all distributed ledgers are blockchains.

Advantages of Distributed Ledger Technology (DLT):

* These ledgers are harder to attack because all of the distributed copies need to be attacked simultaneously for an attack to be successful.

* These ledgers also reduce operational inefficiencies, speed up the amount of time transaction takes to complete, and are automated, and therefore function 24/7, all of which reduce overall costs for the entities that use them.

* These ledgers provide for an easy flow of information, which makes an audit trail easy to follow for accountants when they conduct reviews of financial statements.

Disadvantages of Distributed Ledger Technology (DLT):

* It is complex and difficult to implement and maintain.

* DLT processes may lead to slower processing capabilities or higher costs of use. Some DLTs such as Bitcoin require a significant amount of energy to maintain the network and process transactions.

* It remains risky due to lack of regulation.

Uses of Distributed Ledger Technology (DLT):

*   It enables secure, transparent and decentralized transactions without the need for central authority.

*   It can be used to create a secure and tamper-proof digital identity for individuals, as the technology can provide a reliable way to verify identities and prevent theft.

*   It can be used to create a secure and transparent voting system that can prevent voter fraud and ensure the integrity of the voting process.

*   DLT allows for smart contracts, agreements that automatically execute or complete based on prevailing conditions.

*   It can be used to record property transactions, creating a tamper-proof and transparent record of ownership and transfer of property.

Distributed Ledger Technology (DLT) is becoming necessary in modern businesses and enterprises that need to ensure accuracy in financial reporting, manage supply chains, prevent fraud, and identify inefficiencies.

Mining in Cryptocurrency:

Mining is a way of generating new units of a coin or token by solving computer problems with computers. This helps validate transactions and maintain the security of a decentralized network. In fact, different cryptocurrencies have different mining processes rules. Mining cryptocurrency can involve owning specialized hardware. Mining is the decentralized mathematically intensive computational process by which CRYPTOCURRENCY tokens are created and blockchain LEDGER is maintained and secured. Mining is an essential aspect of most cryptocurrencies.

Mining helps to control inflation for a CRYPTOCURRENCY because it limits the amount of currency that can be put into circulation at any time. For some blockchain, in order to add blocks to the ledger, transfers must go through a MINING process. Mining is a way of adding transaction records, via blocks, onto a public ledger. Miners are nodes in the network that ensure the transactions in the block are valid. Specifically, they ensure that senders have not already used the funds they want to send to receivers. Once miners finish the verification, they have to ask the network for consent to add the new block to the ledger. In order to do so, they have to follow the consensus mechanisms chosen for the platform.

GROWTH OF DIGITAL LEDGER TECHNOLOGY [DLT] AND BENEFITS BY USING IT:

Digital ledger technology is expected to continue growth and adoption in various sectors around the world. Digital ledger technology has been acclaimed as a solution to many different problems, from economic risks present in financial services to extenuating insurance fraud. An increase in investment in private blockchain distributed ledger technology across the globe is expected to propel the tremendous growth of the blockchain distributed ledger market.

The main benefits of using digital ledger technology are as follows:

* Transparency – Digital ledger technology furnishes information to all participants.

* Data integrity – Digital ledger technology has a high level of integrity, as consensus among participants is needed to alter data blocks.

* Efficiency – Digital ledger technology can boost listing, trading and settlement efficiency through decentralization, access information and real-time transaction execution, and by easing payment processing, fund transfers and the exercise of contractual rights.

* Disintermediation – Digital ledger technology-based solutions can foster direct access to primary and secondary markets with peer-to-peer models, decreasing the need for intermediaries and, in turn, reducing costs and counterparty risks.

CHAPTER 7

DECENTRALIZED FINANCE [DEFI]

Decentralized finance is an emerging financial technology that challenges the current centralized banking system. It eliminates the fees that banks and other financial companies charge for using their services and promotes the use of per-to-peer transactions. This is a decentralized financial system more suitable for small / medium businesses in developing countries than a traditional financial banking system with centralized system with intermediaries or third parties. In crypto space, DeFi is one of the crucial aspects to create a completely new independent economic financial system.

Decentralized finance (DeFi) is a blockchain based form of finance. The public can obtain financial services without relying on centralized intermediaries. Unlike a bank [centralized bank], DeFi is a trustless, that is no central authority to control. The contracts in blockchain technology allow cryptocurrency to exist as a decentralized financial system for the global community. In fact, DeFi is transforming global financial services and replacing the centralized financial system.

Decentralized Finance (DeFi) is also known as OPEN FINANCE. It furnishes a broad range of financial services which include CREDIT and or SAVINGS and or INSURANCE in a decentralized manner. Decentralized finance is built on decentralized blockchains. Decentralized blockchains have decentralized architecture, decentralized governance, and decentralized trust. Decentralized finance relies upon contract blockchains, of which ETHEREUM is widely used.

There are leading companies in the growing field of Decentralized Finance which would transform the global financial systems – Coinbase Global, IBM, Meta Platform, Canaan and many others.

Uses of Decentralized Finance (DeFi):

* A peer-to-peer DeFi transaction is where two parties agree to exchange cryptocurrency for goods or services without a third party involved.

* In DeFi, peer-to-peer can meet an individual's loan needs, an algorithm would match peers that agree on the lender's terms, and a loan is issued. Payments from peer-to-peer are made via a decentralized application, or dAPP, and follow the same process in the blockchain.

* Peer-to-peer financial transactions are one of the core premises behind decentralized finance. In brief, a peer-to-peer decentralized is where two parties agree to execute cryptocurrency for goods or services without a third party involved.

* Anyone with an Internet connection can access a decentralized finance platform and transactions occur without any geographic restriction.

* Decentralized finance enables any two parties to directly negotiate interest rates and lend money via decentralized network.

* Smart contracts published on a blockchain and records of completed transactions are available for anyone to review but do not reveal your identity.

* Decentralized finance platform doesn't rely upon any centralized financial institutions and are not subject to adversity or bankruptcy. The decentralized nature of decentralized finance protocols mitigates much of this risk.

Cryptocurrency's Decentralized finance [DeFi] in a nutshell:

Decentralized finance [DeFi] has the potential to furnish financial services to billions of unbanked and underbanked people worldwide, enabling them to access loans / save / invest/ transact globally, fostering economic growth and financial independence. By eliminating intermediaries such as banks, decentralized finance [DeFi] can offer lower fees and faster transactions compared to traditional financial systems, making it more cost-effective and user-friendly. With its open-source nature and permissionless access, decentralized finance [DeFi]can foster the development of innovative financial products and services tailored to specific needs and markets, allowing for increased customization and personalization.

As the decentralized finance [DeFi] ecosystem continues to grow, we can expect increased collaboration and interoperability between different blockchain networks, leading to a more connected and seamless user experience. As decentralized finance [DeFi] gains mainstream attention, regulatory frameworks will likely be developed to furnish clarity and protection for users and investors, further legitimizing the industry and encouraging adoption.

Cryptocurrency's decentralized finance will transform the global financial system in years to come. Cryptocurrency has the potential to promote financial inclusion by making financial services accessible to people worldwide where individuals who don't have banking accounts. With decentralize nature of cryptocurrency will furnish financial services, making it possible for those people to participate in the global financial system. This will eventually promote economic growth in countries around the globe.

We find there is the potential to transform the future of the global financial system in significant ways. Cryptocurrency's decentralized nature, security, and potential for financial innovation make it a transformative force in global finance. In essence, cryptocurrency will play a vital role in the global financial system, and it will play a significant role in transforming the future of global financial sector.

The most significant development in cryptocurrency is the rise of decentralized finance [DeFi] which is an emerging financial system built on blockchain technology that allows for peer-to-peer transactions without intermediaries such as banks. In brief, decentralized finance [DeFi] has created opportunities for financial innovation and has the potential to challenge the present financial systems around the world.

The future of decentralized finance [DeFi] promises immense opportunities for growth, innovation, and financial inclusion. As it continues to progress, it has the potential to revolutionize the way we access and interact with financial services, ultimately empowering individuals and businesses worldwide.

DECENTRALIZATION:

Decentralization is the process by which the activities of an organization, particularly those regarding planning and decision-making, are distributed or delegated away from a central authoritative location or group and given to smaller factions within it. In short, decentralization is the transfer of power, authority, control, and decision-making away from categorized entities to a larger distributed network.

The decentralized network's goal is to create a trustless system where the level of trust needed between network participants is minimal. Decentralization is crucial to blockchain and cryptocurrency. Users can transfer funds and make payments without going through a financial institution via the bitcoin network. The blockchain is not owned or operated by a single entity. It is kept decentralized via a network of operations called 'MINERS' who run the network by processing and validating transactions.

Core principles of decentralization are- autonomy, transparency, censorship – resistance, and privacy are the heart of Bitcoin, Ethereum, and most other public blockchains. These public blockchains operate as open networks. Anyone with an Internet connection can access the network and its ecosystem of applications built on them.

The diagram illustrates the comparison of CENTRALIZED SYSTEM versus DECENTRALIZED SYSTEM

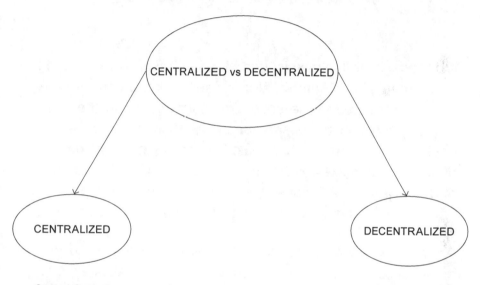

CENTRALIZED vs DECENTRALIZED

CENTRALIZED

Central Control

Authoritarian

Control & Accountability

Hierarchy Decision-making

Little Freedom

Fast Execution

Coordinates

Decisive

Uniformity

DECENTRALIZED

Distributed Control

Delegation Decision-making

Participative

Democratization

Flexible to Adaptation

Facilitates Diversification

Considerable Freedom

Evolutionary

Emergent

CHAPTER 8

CENTRAL BANK DIGITAL CURRENCY [CBDC]

It is digital based money issued by a central bank rather than a commercial bank and is also a liability of the central bank and denominated in the sovereign currency, as in the case with physical banknotes and coins. CBDC is a form of central bank electronic money that could be used by households and businesses to make payments. In essence, the main objective of CBDC is to provide consumers and businesses with privacy, transferability, convenience, accessibility, and financial security.

A central bank digital currency is also known as digital fiat currency or digital base money in the financial world. This is issued by a central bank rather than by a commercial bank. It is also a liability of the central bank denominated in the sovereign currency, as is the case with physical banknotes / coins. It is a form of central bank electronic money that could be used by households and businesses to make payment. However, the central bank DIGITAL currency is NOT well-defined. In brief, CBDC differs from VIRTUAL CURRENCY / CRYPTOCURRENCY.

The following central banks have launched a CBDC namely,

* **The Central bank of the Bahamas**

* **The Eastern Caribbean Central Bank**

* **The Central Bank of Nigeria**

* **The Bank of Jamaica**

* **People's Bank of China**

* **The Reserve Bank of India**

* **Bank of Russia**

Some countries have issued or have considered issuing cryptocurrencies. The countries include:

* **Venezuela**

* **The Marshall Islands**

Central bank digital currency has two categories of central bank money, retail and wholesale.

Retail bank money is the money people have in their wallets or purses. Wholesale bank money is used by community banks for payment clearance and settlements. Retail central bank digital currency has e-money. This is electronic currency wherein the central bank in effect manages a centralized payment system linked to electronic wallets that reside on prepaid cards, smartphones or other electronic devices. The other version is an account based central bank digital currency. In this system, individuals and businesses can access central bank accounts. Here, the central bank manages the payment system with the public. The central digital bank currency payment system with decentralized verifications mechanism managed by the central bank or its authorized agents through a decentralized mechanism that relies on public consensus.

There are two types of retail CBDC. They differ in how individual users access and use their currency.

* **Token-based retail CBDC are accessible with private keys or public keys or both. This method of validation allows users to execute transactions anonymously.**

* **Account-based retail CBDC requires digital identification to access an account.**

Central bank digital currencies are designed to be similar to cryptocurrencies, but they may not require blockchain technology or consensus mechanisms.

Advantages and disadvantages of Central Bank Digital Currency:

Advantages:

Central bank digital currency furnishes more transactions efficient way than cash, making payments cheaper and quicker.

Central bank digital currency can be serviced as a backdrop to private sector managed payment systems, avoiding a breakdown of the payment infrastructure during a crisis of confidence.

Central bank digital currency helps increase financial inclusion, providing low-income householders and those in sparsely populated areas easy access to digital payments and other financial products and services.

Central bank digital currency has the potential to ease the zero lower bound constraint on monetary policy.

Central bank digital currency brings informal economic activity out of the shadow, thereby broadening the tax base and reducing tax evasion, which adds up to higher tax revenue for the government.

Disadvantages:

Central bank digital currency has risk in digital or web based as it is inclined to technological vulnerabilities. For example, hacking.

Central bank digital currency could, depending upon its structure, put the government in direct competition with the private sector in the provision of payment and financial services.

Central bank digital currency could end up precipitating the very risk – financial instability.

Countries in the world with CENTRAL BANK DIGITAL CURRENCIES [CBDC]:

The Bahamas [Sand Dollar]
China [e-CNY]
Nigeria [e-Naira]
Jamaica [JamDex]
India [Digital Rupee]
Russia [Digital Ruble]
Antigua & Barbuda
Dominica
Grenada

Montserrat
St. Kitts & Nevis
Saint Lucia
St. Vincent and the Grenadians [DCash]
Sweden
Ukraine
The United States of America
Tunisia
Venezuela
Marshall Islands
Senegal
United Arab Emirates
Ghana
Malaysia
Singapore
Thailand

CHAPTER 9

COUNTRIES WHERE CRYPTOCURRENCIES ARE IN CIRCULATION

*Vietnam
*Philippines
*Ukraine
*India
*USA
*Pakistan
*Brazil
*Thailand
*Russia
*China
*Nigeria
*Turkey
*Argentina
*Morocco
*UK
*Ecuador
*Kenya
*Indonesia
*UAE
Singapore
*Venezuela
*South Africa
*Germany
*Canada

Popular Cryptocurrencies around the globe:

Bitcoin (BTC)
Ethereum (ETH)
Tether (USDT)
Binance Coin (BNB)
USD Coin (USDC)

World' largest EXCHAGE PLATFORMS for Cryptocurrencies:

*BITCOIN
*COINBASE
*KRAKEN
*KUCOIN
*Bybit

2023 Top CRYPTOCURRENCIES in the WORLD:

*Bitcoin
*Ethereum (ETH)
*Tether
*Biance
*U. S. Dollar coin (USDC)
*XRP
*Lido DAO
*Aptos (Apt)
*Compound (Comp)
*Ripple
*Render Token (RNDR)
*Singularity Net (AGIX)
*Injective (INJ)
*Conflux (CFX)

CHAPTER 10

FUTURE OF GLOBAL FINANCIAL SYSTEMS

Cryptocurrency in terms of Global financial system:

Cryptocurrency is having an enormous impact on the global financial system. It is challenging traditional institutions and creating new opportunities for financial innovation. In other words, the rise of cryptocurrency has been driven by several factors such as decentralization, security, and potential for innovation.

One of the most significant developments has been the rise of decentralized finance [DeFi]. This has created several new opportunities for financial innovation and has the potential to challenge the traditional financial system. In essence, cryptocurrency has disrupted traditional financial institutions by providing an alternative to the centralized financial system. The global financial system encompasses financial markets, and current markets in the world economy. Besides these, exchange rates and capital flows among those nations wrap them together. However, they face more problems than benefits. In brief, developing nations feel that they are manipulated in favor of the developed nations around the world. We also see fintech, decentralized finance [DeFi] are even central bank digital currency [CBDC] and other new advanced technologies will pave the way to transform the global financial system.

Blockchain technology and Digital Ledger Technology [DLT] in terms of Global Financial System:

We see that cryptocurrency and digital ledger technology will become a major player in the global financial system and that it will play a crucial role in shaping the future of money and finance. Blockchain and digital ledger technology are advancing rapidly and as more people adopt them. In fact, blockchain technologies are connecting the global financial system. They are easily interoperable, efficient, affordable and accessible. They can reduce the cost and time of cross-border payments. In essence, blockchain technology reduces fraud, ensures quick and secure transactions, trading and it helps to manage risk within the interconnected global financial system. With blockchain technology anyone can connect financial infrastructure anywhere in the world. Digital ledger technology is a decentralized database that records transactions in a secure and transparent manner. It has the potential to revolutionize the global financial system by enabling faster, cheaper, and more secure transactions.

When it comes to digital ledger technology, it decentralizes critical data and enables an entirely new financial system where capital flows without the need for traditional intermediaries such as banks. Digital ledger technology offers the potential for tracking various stages of trade and financial transactions.

The era of cash / credit card/ debit card etc. are coming to an end and that of CBDC – Central Bank Digital Currencies has already begun with DIGITAL payment systems becoming the criterion around the globe. We see many of the global population are gaining access to digital systems. In other words, fintech is transforming the world of finance.

The future of cryptocurrency in global financial systems will be shaped by regulations as the role of government regulators in the world will be a foremost important factor in the future of cryptocurrency. Central banks and government regulators have their eyes on this growing trend of crypto space. There will be an impact on the development of global financial system in terms of crypto space in the years to come. Blockchain will play a crucial role.

The future of global financial systems has intellectually impacted by cryptocurrencies. For instance, transactions, financial inclusion, and funding have been altered by their cross-border nature, decentralization, and potential innovation. In essence, cryptocurrencies can enable financial inclusion by creating open democratic financial systems that are global, open source and accessible to all who have access to the Internet, regardless of nationality, ethnicity, race, gender and socioeconomic class.

We see most of the global financial institutions carry corruption and incompetence on a grand scale. It is in a state of upheaval disrupting honest human enterprise the systems. When bitcoin was created, it showed that building a non-hackable system of rules utilizing software known as BLOCKCHAIN is possible without anyone making them work. It showed that the digital system could be applied to law and private ownership of labor, merchandise, property and financial institutions and how they work. Bitcoin showed that users of all systems can deal honestly and openly between two individuals and that administrator is unnecessary. In essence, Bitcoin is an immutable system of truth that can be utilized to conduct transactions around the globe without ever being exposed to the monopolies that have previously served as go between taking fees. We find decentralized finance (DeFi) is challenging the need for bureaucracies in financial services. There is a software NFT [Non-Fungible Tokens] that has systems of rules to eliminate issues and deal honestly and truthfully with others without the need for many bureaucracies. BLOCKCHAIN TECHNOLOGY will get rid of most of the abusive monopolies. It is estimated that 1.7 billion people globally still do not have access to banking institutions or cannot afford the banking services. Now, they depend on cryptocurrency to join free commerce.

Global financial systems, particularly in the banking industry, were the first to recognize the threat of BITCOIN and then the potential of BLOCKCHAIN TECHNOLOGY to transform the industry. The DIGITAL CURRENCY does not carry the COST of handling cash and that is traceable as it moves through the FINANCILAL SYSTEM.

One of the primary challenges that the United States faces is that it's decentralized in the distribution of power and decision-making. Each county and each state will come up with its own rules for how to implement or use blockchain technology.

Ninety-five (95%) of the global population has access to CRYPTOCURRENCIES. In other words, they can buy and trade new financial products. In essence every individual could start using a sovereign identity [sovereign identity refers to an individual's ability to control and manage their own digital identity, instead of relying on third parties to do so on their behalf. In other words, a sovereign identity system, which may include personal information, credentials, and other types of data. These identities are usually stored on a decentralized platform, such as blockchain, which allows the public to control and access their identity information without relying upon a central authority. In essence, the goal of sovereign identity is to give individuals more control over their personal data and to enable them to securely and privately interact with various systems and services online. Lately we see Decentralized finance (DeFi) is counterbalanced to transform the global financial systems. Many countries around the globe are currently developing new blockchain-based technologies, platforms, and applications that offer alternatives to traditional financial services. In essence, many of these businesses are transforming the way people store, transfer, and manage their money, making finance accessible, secure, and efficient. These businesses are being created to make decentralized (DeFi) a reality for people around the globe. The growing ecosystem of cryptocurrency is making headways into the global financial systems. Globally, the numerous users of various cryptocurrencies have grown more than 100 million. As Blockchain technology develops, more private and public sectors around the world acknowledge and accept cryptocurrency as a viable global financial system.

About five years ago, the deputy governor of Sweden's central bank, predicted the end of money. She told 'if you extrapolate current trends, the last note will have been handed back to the Riksbank (Sweden) by year 2030.' What she meant was, the use of paper currency to carry out commercial transactions in Sweden would cease at that point. As a matter of fact, the Sveriges Riksbank was the world's first central bank and among the first to issue currency banknotes. Now we see smartphones allow us to conduct banking and financial transactions no matter where we are. Consumers around the globe are faced with a range of important transformations, which they are adopting with varying degrees of enthusiasm depending on their age, technical savvy, and socioeconomic status. Companies / businesses around the world are having to adapt as well. All these revolutionary transformations in finance seemed to have been heralded. In brief, there are numerous cryptocurrencies available in the world. These currencies have been heralded as a replacement for fiat currency. In this scenario, cryptocurrencies would disrupt the global financial system so completely that they will supplant all conventional currencies, even the dollar, sterling, yen, yuan etc.

CHAPTER 11

GLOBAL VIEW OF STATUS OF CRYPTO SPACE

ANTIGUA & BARBADA:

Population- 101,489

Business culture Characteristics- Handshaking is the normal greeting for acquaintances and formal introduction. Business cards are exchanged.

Literacy- 99%

Economy- Dual island -tourism & construction driven economy – limited water supply.

GDP per capita- $19,100

Regulation- There are no limits for foreign control investments and ownership. Foreign investors may hold up to 100 % of an investment. Mostly legal investment.

Cryptocurrency- Financial innovation in cryptocurrency & blockchain technologies. Bitcoin and bitcoin cash is accepted.

SAINT KITTS:

Population- 54,817

Business Culture Characteristics- Materials possessions are important. Education matters greatly.

Literacy- 98%

Economy- High-income, tourism-based economy. Growing offshore financial & telecommunications hub.

GDP per capita- $26,500

Regulation- Mostly legal investment.

Cryptocurrency- There is a legal framework for cryptocurrencies that will ensure that each provider participating in cryptocurrency services must register with the government.

MONTSERRAT:

Population- 5,440

Business culture characteristics- The people are usually friendly & relaxed.

Literacy- 97%

Economy- High-income economy, geothermal & solar power.

GDP per capita- $34,000

Regulation- Yet to enact laws governing cryptocurrencies.

Cryptocurrency- 'Skilling' is the cryptocurrency exchange.

DOMINICA:

Population- 74,656

Business culture Characteristics- Dealings are formal. Punctuality is expected.

Literacy- 93.7%

Economy- Emerging ecotourism.

GDP per capita- $10,900

Regulation- Yet to enact laws governing cryptocurrencies.

Cryptocurrency- Cryptocurrency transactions in Dominica are impossible to hack as these are specialized encryption techniques.

SAINT LUCIA:

Population- 167,591

Business culture Characteristics- Influenced by African, East Indian, French & English heritage.

Literacy- 90%

Economy- Tourism-based economy

GDP per capita- $13,000

Regulation- Mostly legal investment.

Cryptocurrency- Cryptocurrency is legal. Cryptocurrency exchange platforms are: Binance, Kraken, Coinmama.

SAINT VINCENT & THE GRENADIANS:

Population- 100, 804

Business Culture Characteristics- Easy going people. Informal & relaxed lifestyle.

Literacy- 96%

Economy- Upper-middle-income economy, agriculture & tourism.

GDP per capita- $13, 700

Regulation- Government has not passed any legislation.

Cryptocurrency- They are participating in implementing. cryptocurrency as a fiat currency.

GRENADA:

Population- 114, 299

Business culture Characteristics- They are serious about their jobs.

Literacy- 98.6%

Economy- Tourism.

GDP per capita- $13,700

Regulation- Does not have any specific legislation to regulate cryptocurrencies.

Cryptocurrency- Binance and Kraken are the cryptocurrency exchange platforms.

THE BAHAMAS:

Population- 388,508

Business Culture Characteristics- Punctuality in business meetings & formal attire.

Literacy- 95%

Economy- High-income tourism & financial services economy.

GDP per capita- $30,200

Regulation- Mostly legal investment.

Cryptocurrency- Cryptocurrency accepted. Cryptocurrency exchange platforms are: Binance, Kraken, Coinmama.

EL SALVADOR:

Population- 6,602,370

Business Culture Characteristics- Business is conducted after a relationship has been established.

Literacy- 89.9%

Economy- Service-based economy

GDP- $9,100

Regulation- No legal framework

Cryptocurrency- Cryptocurrency is the official legal currency. They adopted bitcoin as their currency in 2021. They believe that bitcoin is the path to financial freedom.

VENEZUELA:

Population- 30,518,260

Business Culture Characteristics- Arrive on time for meetings. A standard professional greeting is a handshake. Venezuela is a country comprised of diverse people often characterized by their outgoing and friendly nature. This can be seen in how they greet each other and their body language. Venezuelans are known to stand in close proximity and to use hand-gestures, even touching, when in conversation. Greeting with two kisses to the cheek is common for both men and women, although men only kiss women. Men typically greet each other with a firm handshake and some cases a hug depending upon the status of the person. Venezuela is a patriarchal society that displays machismo, the notion of masculine superiority. As a results, there are distinct differences between the social expectations and the treatment of men and women in society. The belief in traditional gender roles is still prevalent. However, the ideal of machismo is being confronted as more women continue to join the workforce and North American culture penetrates. Venezuela has a strong defined socioeconomic class structure that is often divided along gender and ethnicity. The Venezuelan business style is casual, with most of the address being informal. The Venezuelans have a strong sense of independence and do not feel compelled to abide by the rules at all times. Overall, their laid-back attitude translates into the business environment. Patriotism toward their country is what most Venezuelans feel. Drawing up contracts in Venezuela is never a reciprocal situation. Most of them are reluctant to commit things to writing yet would appreciate it greatly if the information that they receive is specified.

Literacy- 97.5%

Economy- Privately-owned and state-owned, petroleum

GDP- $7,704

Regulation- Mostly legal investment.

Cryptocurrency- OnixCoin, DashVenezeula, BolivarCoin, ArepaCoin are the most cryptocurrencies.

ECUADOR:

Population- 17,483,326

Business Culture Characteristics- Spending time cultivating relationships.

Literacy- 93.6%

Economy- Major banana exporter

GDP- $10,700

Regulation-Cryptocurrency is not a means of payment.

Cryptocurrency- Transaction takes place in a fully decentralized market.

ARGENTINA:

Population- 40,621,847

Business Culture Characteristics- Argentine people tend to differ from other Latin Americans in the way they conduct business. They are seen resourceful, highly educated, and motivated to form business networks and boost the exchange between Argentina and the rest of the world. Business style in Argentina is colored by the mixed heritage that it has. Generally, they are intensely competitive, and this has been one of the redeeming factors that have increased the internationalization of its markets. Family oriented. Personal relationships. Loyalty to individual people. High value placed on educational level. The Argentines emphasize the individual's role in society and view the individual who is independent as capable. This affects the business culture, since the Argentines perceive one who takes orders from another as weak and inadequate. Acts of generosity which manifest in helping someone in need, are considered an exercise of free will. The difference between the residents of Buenos Aires and the rest of the country is also an aspect of culture that should be noted. When dealing with an Argentine, it is important to note their frankness in voicing out their opinions, though they take extreme care in being diplomatic. Their warm nature and friendliness are seen in situations when they try to establish a personal relationship prior to business dealing. It is also important to note the concept of space and time in dealing in Argentina. Most Argentines maintain little physical distance between speakers and tend to broach personal issues pertaining to the family in their conversation. Time is considered to be an asset to be enjoyed rather than utilized, and most Argentines take this to be useful to establish relationships and to clarify situations better. The role of the family in Argentine life is to be emphasized. Family is deemed central to the life of the average citizen, and filial piety and bonds to elders are cherished. However, one of the main perils with working in Argentina would be in dealing with nepotism. Most positions are filled with family members first, and while there are specific rules which limit such incidents, this occurrence is significantly less than in other Latin American countries.

Literacy- 99%

Economy- Large diversified economy.

GDP- $21,500

Regulation- Mostly legal investment

Cryptocurrency- Cryptocurrency is accepted. Cryptocurrency exchange platforms are: Binance, Bitex, SatoshiTango.

BRAZIL:

Population- 218,689,757

Business Culture Characteristics- It is characterized by openness. Patience & flexibility. The Brazilian culture is one of the world's most varied and diverse cultures. It is derived from influences from Portuguese, African, indigenous, and other European cultures. The family structure and vales are very important in Brazil, with large, extended families being the norm. Brazilians tend to be affectionate, tactile people with a smaller sense of personal space. There is a level of informality in how Brazilians greet and address each other. Shaking hands, hugs, and kisses on the cheek are common greetings through women tend to touch more and greet with kisses. Brazilians usually address teachers, doctors, priests, and other professionals using their titles followed by their name. Body language and terms of address also vary with an individual's social standing. Brazilian culture has class distinctions based upon one's socioeconomic status and ethnic background. Brazil's business community is highly educated, and a significant portion of the population is well versed in English as well as another foreign language. The expectation when conducting business in Brazil is to deal with the individual first, not the business. A relationship will need to be established, as Brazilian prefer to take their time to get to know one another before committing to a contract. Punctuality at events and dinners is expected. In addition, formal dress is the norm within the business setting. When in doubt, it is considered better to over-dress than to appear too casual in appearance.

Literacy- 94.3%

Economy- Industrial led economy

GDP per capita- $14,600

Regulation- cryptocurrency accepted.

Cryptocurrency- Mostly legal investment. Binance, FoxBit are the exchange platforms.

COLOMBIA:

Population: 4,336,454

Business Culture Characteristics: Tends to be quite formal. Prefer doing business in person.

Literacy: 95%

Economy: Consistent growth

GDP: $14,600

Regulation: Not yet regulated

Cryptocurrency: Cryptocurrency exchange platforms are: Bybit, eToro, Binance, Gate.io.

PERU:

Population- 32,440,172

Business Culture Characteristics- Hierarchical with decision-making done from top.

Literacy- 94.5%

Economy- Upper-middle-income

GDP- $12,500

Regulation- Mostly legal investment.

Cryptocurrency- Binance, Kraken, Coinmama are the exchange platforms for cryptocurrencies.

COSTA RICA:

Population: 5,256,612

Business Culture Characteristics: Building relationships & trust is crucial. Flexibility & patience are important. Dress smartly.

Literacy: 97.9%

Economy: Trade-based upper-middle-income

GDP: $21,200

Regulation: Mostly legal investment

Cryptocurrency: Legal. Cryptocurrency exchange platforms are: eToro, Skilling, Binance.

CUBA:

Population: 10,985,974

Business Culture Characteristics: They work around regularity restrictions.

Literacy: 99%

Economy: State-run planned economy

GDP: $12,300

Regulation: Central bank issues regulation for digital asset service providers

Cryptocurrency: Central bank recognizes bitcoin.

GUATEMALA:

Population: 17,980,803

Business Culture Characteristics: Make appointments before visiting. Punctuality. Hierarchical business environment. Persona; connections for successful business.

Literacy: 83.5%

Economy: Growing central American economy

GDP: $8,900

Regulation: Yet to legalizing cryptocurrency

Cryptocurrency:

BOLIVIA:

Population: 12,186,079

Business Culture Characteristics: Bolivian government is eager to attract foreign investment. Most members of Bolivia's private sector are experienced businesspersons with ample direct exposure to United States and West European customs and procedures.

Very formal. Treat those in authority with particular respect. Spend time cultivating relationships.

Literacy: 93.8%

Economy: Resources-rich economy

GDP: $8,100

Regulation: Banned

Cryptocurrency: Banned

CHILE:

Population: 18,549,457

Business Culture Characteristics: Formal & conservative appearance is important. Business structures are hierarchical & decision-making is made at the top.

Literacy: 84%

Economy: Export driven, leader of copper

Regulation: Mostly legal investment

Cryptocurrency: Cryptocurrency exchange platforms are: Binance, Krake, eToro.

HONDURAS:

Population: 9,571,352

Business Culture Characteristics: Business negotiations tend to be slower. More emphasis on relationships.

Literacy: 88%

Economy: Second fastest growing central American economy

GDP: $5,600

Regulation: Yet to create a regulatory framework

Cryptocurrency: Cryptocurrency exchange platforms are: Binance, Krake, Coinmama.

PARAQUAY:

Population: 7,439,863

BSINESS Culture Characteristics: Generally conservative. Cleanliness is expected.

Literacy: 94%

Economy: Upper middle-income south American economy

GDP: $13,700

Regulation: No regulatory framework

Cryptocurrency: Cryptocurrency exchange platforms are: Binance, Kraken, Coinmama.

KENYA:

Population- 57,052,004

Business Culture Characteristics- Informal, open, shaking hands, exchange business cards.

Literacy- 82.6%

Economy- Third largest sub-Saharan economy. Strong agriculture, emerging services and tourism industries.

GDP per capita: $4,700

Regulation- Mostly legal investment.

Cryptocurrency- They have the mobile payment system-M-PESA which is used by 90% of all Kenyans – to illustrate that digital banking is possible with high rates of poverty and relatively poor infrastructure. Cryptocurrency exchange platforms are: Avatrade, FXGT, FBS, TickMill, JustMarkets, FxPro

TANZANIA:

Population: 65,642,682

Business Culture Characteristics: Friendly & easygoing, punctuality is expected.

Literacy: 81%

Economy: Emerging low middle-income

GDP: $2,600

Regulation: Restricted

Cryptocurrency: Not legal. Cryptocurrency exchange platforms are: Binance, Kraken, Coinmama.

TUNISIA:

Population: 11, 976,182

Business Culture Characteristics: Personal relationships, trust, hierarchical.

Literacy: 82%

Economy: Lower middle-income

GDP: $10,400

Regulation: Cryptocurrency banned

Cryptocurrency: not recognized

SOUTH AFRICA:

Population-

Business Culture Characteristics- Conducting business dealings in South Africa is rather tedious. South Africa is a country with a very diverse culture rich in ethnic and language differences among population. The majority of the population is comprised of the white, colored, Asian/Indian, and Native African ethnic groups. In terms of language, there are eleven official languages spoken, and these tend to be vernacular or dialects. Conducting business dealings in South Africa is rather tedious. Most Africans do not stand on formality, and though that connotes a relaxed attitude, they do not fall into that category either. Personal matters are kept separate from business dealings. Similarly, it is considered impolite to discuss business at home. Some of the informality can be seen in the way people are most commonly addressed by their first name in business settings. Also, prefixes such as Mr. and Mrs. and professional titles such as Dr are not commonly used. Most business is conducted in English. However, special note must be taken of the accent and undertones of speech. For example, the use of overly diplomatic language by a foreigner may be interpreted as a lack of commitment or dishonesty. As such, it is preferred to speak plainly and directly in many instances. It is also preferred that hard selling is not used as a tactic. Such behavior would be perceived negatively. Instead, a friendlier approach that focuses on the relationship would allow for better negotiations. In terms of gestures, handshaking and backslapping are the norm greeting or doing introduction. Suth Africa is conservative society and dress should be formal and appropriate for the occasion, particularly business settings.

Literacy- 87%

Economy-

GDP- $13,300

Regulation- Mostly legal investment.

Cryptocurrency- Cryptocurrency exchange platforms are: Binance, Coinbase, Coinmama, Kraken

NIGERIA:

Population- 230,842,743

Business Culture Characteristics- Personal relationships, adaptability, flexibility & patience.

Literacy- 62%

Economy- Larger African Market economy, Major oil exporter.

GDP- $4,900

Regulation- Mostly legal investment.

Cryptocurrency- Cryptocurrency exchange platforms are: Binance, Luno, Quidax, NairaEx, Kraken, Coinbase, Bybit, KuCoin.

AUSTRALIA:

Population- 26,461,166

Business Culture Characteristics- Australians tend to be friendly and easy-going, this behavior does not carry over to business relations. Most expect a code of etiquette with emphasis on the verbal as well as nonverbal aspects. It is considered appropriate to offer your business card, but you might not receive on in return because most Australians do not carry name cards. It is customary to shake hands when greeting, as it is at the conclusion of a meeting. It is also acceptable for people to introduce themselves without waiting to be introduced and most Australians would perceive this as informal and outgoing.

Literacy- 99%

Economy- Strong financial sector, energy investor.

GDP per capita- $49,800

Regulation- Mostly legal investment.

Cryptocurrency- Cryptocurrency accepted. Cryptocurrency exchange platforms are: Bybit, Swyfix, Coinspot, Coinjar, Luno, eToro, Binance, Kucoin, Phemex, Cointree

TURKEY:

Population- 83,593,483

Business Culture Characteristics- Friendly & sincere, value personal relationships, loyal to business, negotiating takes time-be patient.

Literacy- 96.7%

Economy- Upper-middle-income

GDP per capita- $31,500

Regulation- Mostly legal investment.

Cryptocurrency- Binance, OKX, Kraken are the cryptocurrency exchange platforms.

MALTA:

Population- 467,138

Business Culture Characteristics- Business communications & business etiquette.

Literacy- 94.9%

Economy- Higher income, tourism

GDP per capita- $44,700

Regulations- Mostly legal investment.

Cryptocurrency- They embrace blockchain technology They support international blockchain and cryptocurrency related companies. Cryptocurrency exchange platforms are: eToro, Uphold, Bybit, OKX.

SINGAPORE:

Population- 5,975,383

Business Culture Characteristics- Relationship-oriented, hierarchical, negotiations at slow pace, require trust & loyalty, observe etiquette.

Literacy- 97.5%

Economy- Higher income, service-based economy

GDP per capita- $106,000

Regulations- Mostly legal investment.

Cryptocurrency- Singapore's central bank launched a project to use the blockchain technology for its interbank payments. Singapore has a modern digital identity system that could easily be connected to a blockchain. They have digital identity to IoT sensors that optimize public records. Cryptocurrency exchange platforms are: Phemex, Binance, BYDFi, PrimeXBT, Coinbase, BingX.

INDONESIA:

Population- 279,476,346

Business Culture Characteristics- Diversity of people, family-oriented, high value on social harmony, hierarchical.

Literacy- 96%

Economy- One of the faster growing economies, upper-middle-income

GDP per capita- $11,900

Regulation- Mostly legal investment.

Cryptocurrency- Tadpole, Xaurius, BotXCoin, Meong, Toko Token, Zipmex Token are the cryptocurrency exchange platforms.

HONG KONG:

Population- 7,288,176

Business Culture Characteristics- Exchange business cards, long-term business relationships, hierarchical structure, dress codes.

Literacy-

Economy- High-income, tourism & service-based economy

GDP per capita- $60,000

Regulation- Mostly legal investment.

Cryptocurrency- Cryptocurrency exchange platforms are Binance, Coinmama, Huobi

TAIWAN:

Population- 23,588,613

Business Culture Characteristics- Hierarchical structure, respect for authority, ranks & status, harmony.

Literacy- 98.5%

Economy- Higher income & technologically

GDP per capita- $47,800

Regulation- Mostly legal investment.

Cryptocurrency- Cryptocurrency exchange platforms are: Binance, Kraken, Huobi

CAMBODIA:

Population: 16,891,245

Business Culture characteristics: Conservative, formal dress, punctuality, harmony, seniority.

Literacy: 83%

Economy: One of the fastest growing economies, Tourism

GDP: $4,400

Regulation: No regulating framework

Cryptocurrency: Legal. Cryptocurrency exchange platforms are: Binance, Kraken, Coinmama.

MALAYSIA:

Population- 34,219,975

Business Culture Characteristics- Hierarchical, teamwork, collaborations.

Literacy- 95%

Economy- Upper-middle-income, high labor productivity.

GDP per capita- $26,300

Regulation- Mostly legal investment.

Cryptocurrency- Binance, Kraken, Coinmama are the cryptocurrency exchange platforms.

MAURITIUS:

Population- 1,309,448

Business Culture Characteristics- Punctual to meetings, shaking hands, exchange business cards.

Literacy- 91.3%

Economy- Upper-middle-income

GDP- $21,000

Regulation-Mostly legal investment.

Cryptocurrency- Binance, Kraken, Coinmama are the cryptocurrency exchange platforms.

BANGALADESH:

Population: 167,184,465

Business Culture Characteristics: Arrive for meetings on time, handshaking, exchange business cards, professionalism is highly valued.

Literacy: 74.9%

Economy: One of the fastest growing economies.

GDP: $5,900

Regulation: Prohibits

Cryptocurrency: Cryptocurrency exchange platforms are: Binance, eToro

NEPAL:

Population: 30,899,443

Business Culture Characteristics: Handshake

Literacy: 76%

Economy: Low-income

GDP: $3,800

Regulation: Banned transaction

Cryptocurrency: Illegal. Cryptocurrency exchange platforms are: Binance, Skilling, Avatrade.

VIETNAM:

Population- 104,799,174

Business Culture Characteristics- Schedule meetings in advance, dress appropriately

Literacy- 95.7%

Economy- Lower-middle-income

GDP- $10,600

Regulation- Mostly legal investment.

Cryptocurrency- Cryptocurrency exchange platforms are BitcoinVN, VBTC, Binance.

CHINA:

Population- 1,413,142,846

Business Culture Characteristics- The Chinese give a lot of importance to value of time and most meetings commence on time. They place a lot of emphasis on precision and detail when designing contracts. They pay close attention to long-standing relationships because it is believed that the culture of each business is better understood by building long-term relationships. It does take a significant amount of time for a business entering China to understand the legal aspects as well as the culture in negotiating deals. In establishing business deals, the business that invests in understanding and appreciating the Chinese culture succeeds. On the other side, Chinese understand the cultural differences and would not expect foreigners to get fully acclimatized to their tradition. They would go with their assessment of their partners rather than the custom alignment. In order to prevent loss face, most Chinese would prefer to work on a one-on-one basis with the party and not through an intermediary. In terms of nonverbal communications, it would help to assess the status of the officials who have convened to discuss the contract. Most Chinese meetings are developed to pleasantries in order to wait for the most opportunities moment to discuss formal aspects of the contract or the business. Most Chinese tend to become rigid in posture when their position is in jeopardy.

Literacy- 96.8%

Economy- One of the world's top two economies, manufacturing & exporting.

GDP per capita- $17,600

Regulations- Does not recognize cryptocurrencies as legal tender.

Cryptocurrency- The country has its own form of digital currency called the e-yuan, which has many million users. Cryptocurrency exchange platforms are: OKX, Huobi, Binance, BitFinex, Gate.io, BTCC, CoinEgg, ZB.com

JAPAN:

Population- 123,719,238

Business Culture Characteristics- The Japanese get familiar with the culture of the people whom they deal with. Japanese are very polite and try to accommodate everybody's needs and wishes. When approaching the Japanese, one should take caution in not being too direct, because this would mean that if they are not able to answer or accommodate, they query, that would result in them loosing face in front of the foreign party. Given the level of collectivism in the Japanese society, it translates to such a system in the workplace. Most executives convene as a group, and often it is difficult to determine who is at the top of the hierarchy. Politeness, sensitivity, and good manners form the foundation of businesses in Japan. Being loyal to a business is considered a virtue and many executives spend a number of years with the business. This translates to a long-term relationship with partners in business scenarios. Significant emphasis is placed on the actual interaction with the clients. The Japanese tend to be very formal in their meetings. Time is sacrosanct in Japan, and they would like to be aware of any delays in advance. They prefer formal dress in client meetings and give a lot of importance to business cards. Business cards need to be exchanged during meetings. Accept business cards with respect and keep them safe, as forgetting to pick up their business cards is considered impolite and is considered a proxy for the lack of interest in a long-term relationship.

Literacy-

Economy- Fourth largest trade-oriented economy

GDP per capita- $40,800

Regulation- Mostly legal investment.

Cryptocurrency- Cryptocurrency is accepted. Cryptocurrency exchange platforms are: Binance, bitFlyer, Coincheck.

PHILIPPINES:

Population- 116,434,200

Business Culture Characteristics- Trust, loyalty, conservative approach to decision-making.

Literacy- 96.3%

Economy- Diversified economy, ship building

GDP per capita- $8,100

Regulation- Mostly legal investment.

Cryptocurrency- Binance, OKX, Kraken are the cryptocurrency exchange platforms.

INDIA:

Population- 1,399,179,585

Business Culture Characteristics- Conducting business in India requires considering certain cultural aspects and nuances. The use of the first name for address should be avoided. The usual method used will be press one's palms together in front of the chest and say "Namaste," meaning "Greetings to you." The attitude toward women is one of the respects and the distance between men and women is one of that should be maintained when addressing them.

In conducting business, it would be appropriate to chart the dimensions of contractual agreement in order to have a document to refer to over an extended period of time. Diversity, privacy, punctuality, physical presence is essential.

Literacy- 74.4%

Economy- Largest south Asian economy.

GDP per capita- $6,600

Regulation- Mostly legal investment.

Cryptocurrency- Cryptocurrency exchange platforms are: WazirX, Binance, Coinbase, Coinmama, Unocoin.

PAKISTAN:

Population- 247,653,551

Business Culture Characteristics- It is good to arrive on time. Wait to be introduced. Exchange business cards.

Literacy- 58%

Economy- Lower-middle-income

GDP- $5,200

Regulation- Mostly legal investment.

Cryptocurrency- Cryptocurrency exchange platforms are: Bybit, Binance, OKX, Gate.io, KUCoin.

THAILAND:

Population- 69,794,997

Business Culture Characteristics- Personal relationships, hierarchical, negotiations may be lengthy, business decisions are slow, they respect foreigners.

Literacy- 94.1%

Economy- Upper-middle-income, electronics, automobile manufacturing

GDP- $17,100

Regulation- Mostly legal investment.

Cryptocurrency- Bitkub, SaanG, Binance are the cryptocurrency exchange platforms,

SOUTH KOREA:

Population- 51,966,948

Business Culture Characteristics- Values respect, hierarchical, business cards exchanged.

Literacy- 98%

Economy- Strong export-driven, global healthcare technology., automobile manufacturing.

GDP per capita- $44,200

Regulation- Mostly legal investment.

Cryptocurrency- Binance, Korbit, Upbit are cryptocurrency exchange platforms.

ESTONIA:

Population-1,202,762

Business Culture Characteristics- Characterized by individualism, patriotism, strong work ethics.

Literacy- 99.9%

Economy- Advanced service-based economy

GDP per capita- $38,700

Regulations- Mostly legal investment.

Cryptocurrency- They have embraced blockchain technology. Estonia has digital ID cards for online services and were the first country to offer-e-Residency, a digital identity, available to anyone in the world interested in operating a business online.

Binance, Kraken, Bitpanda are cryptocurrency exchange platforms.

UKRAINE:

Population- 43,306,477

Business Culture Characteristics- Make appointments well in advance, punctuality, arrive on time, personal relationships, hierarchical.

Literacy- 100%

Economy- Lower middle-income economy, major wheat producer & Industrial &energy producer

GDP per capita- $12,900

Regulation- Mostly legal investment.

Cryptocurrency- Kuna, Binance, OKX are the cryptocurrency exchange platforms.

CZECHOSLOVAKIA:

Population- 10,706,242

Business Culture Characteristics- Business is conducted slowly, hierarchical.

Literacy- 99%

Economy- High income, diversified.

GDP- $40,700

Regulation- Mostly legal investment.

Cryptocurrency- Cryptocurrency exchange platforms are: Binance, Kraken, Bitpanda

BELARUS:

Population- 9,383,853

Business Culture Characteristics- Business meetings tend to be low key but formal, personal relationships.

Literacy- 99.8%

Economy- Public debt, fragile private sector.

GDP- $19,800

Regulation- Mostly legal investment.

Cryptocurrency- Cryptocurrency is accepted. Binance, Kraken, Coinmama are cryptocurrency exchange platforms.

RUSSIA:

Population- 141,698,923

Business Culture Characteristics- Characterized by cautions, persistence, strong hierarchical which modestly causes a certain bureaucracy to occur.

Literacy- 99.7%

Economy- Natural resources, energy exporter, oil & gas exporter.

GDP- $28,000

Regulation- Digital currencies cannot be used to pay for any goods & services.

Cryptocurrency- Cryptocurrency exchange platforms are: Bybit, Binance, Gate.io, OKX, KuCoin.

MONGOLIA:

Population: 3,255,468

Business Culture Characteristics: Generous hosts.

Literacy: 99%

Economy: Lower-middle-income

GDP: $11,700

Regulation: Mostly legal investment

Cryptocurrency: Legal. Cryptocurrency exchange platforms are: Binance, Kraken, Coinmama.

GEORGIA:

Population- 4,936,390

Business Culture Characteristics- Business meetings tend to be relatively relaxed affairs.

Literacy- 99.5%

Economy- Transportation & construction

GDP- $15,500

Regulation- Mostly legal investment.

Cryptocurrency-Cryptocurrency is legal. Cryptocurrency exchange platforms are: Binance, Coinmama

SLOVANIA:

Population- 2,099,790

Business Culture Characteristics- Hierarchical, patience, respect in business communications, business meetings are conducted slowly.

Literacy- 99%

Economy- High income

GDP- $40,000

Regulation- Mostly legal investment.

Cryptocurrency- Cryptocurrency exchange platforms are: Bitget, Binance, KuCoin, eToro, Bybit.

LITHUANIA:

Population- 2,555,755

Business Culture Characteristics- Characterized by business communications, business etiquette.

Literacy- 99.8%

Economy- High income

GDP- $39,300

Regulation- Mostly legal investment.

Cryptocurrency- eToro, Uphold, OKX, Bbit, Bitpanda are the cryptocurrency exchange platforms.

SWITZERLAND:

Population- 8,563,760

Business Culture Characteristics- Ese of doing business, business culture is relaxed & polite. Hierarchical in structure, quite conservative in rems of values.

Literacy- 99%

Economy- High income, banking & financial hub.

GDP- $71,000

Regulation- Mostly legal investment.

Cryptocurrency- Binance, OKX, Kraken are the cryptocurrency exchange platforms.

GERMANY:

Population- 84,220,184

Business Culture Characteristics- German managers are experts in their fields and expected to lead others by exhibiting strong and clear leadership skills. Their concept of business dealings involves formal interaction with the clientele where it would be advantageous to the client to be well prepared for the meeting, as Germans generally come well prepared for their meetings. The individual never mentions his / her achievements or offers insight into his / her personal matters. In Germany, t is important that the dealings are made specific, either in writing or verbally. This is specifically because Germans pay attention to detail, and anything that is not specified will be considered in breach of trust.

Germans tend to prefer the formal form of addressing people, and the use of first names should be avoided. For the Germans, greeting is almost always a firm handshake. Ther is significant emphasis placed on the seniority of one employee over another, and this inadvertently also relates to the formality of relationships within the company. Privacy, punctuality, hierarchical, loyalty, professionalism, reliability, business cards are exchanged.

Literacy- 99%

Economy- Leading EU economy, service-based

GDP- $53,200

Regulation- Mostly legal investment.

Cryptocurrency- Binance, Kraken, Bitpanda are the cryptocurrency exchange platforms.

FRANCE:

Population- 68,521,974

Business Culture Characteristics- Business communication is formal & respectful, greetings with handshakes, using titles, punctuality, exchange business cards.

Literacy- 99%

Economy- High income Advanced & Diversified EU economy.

GDP- $45,000

Regulation- Mostly legal investment.

Cryptocurrency- Cryptocurrency exchange platforms are: Binance, Kraken, Bitanda.

ITALY:

Population- 61,021,855

Business Culture Characteristics- Casual workplace relations, hierarchical.

Literacy- 99.3%

Economy- Core EU economy, strong services, manufacturing, tourism

GDP- $41,900

Regulation- Mostly legal investment.

Cryptocurrency- Binanace, Kraken, Bitpanda are the cryptocurrency exchange platforms.

SPAIN:

Population- 47,222,613

Business Culture Characteristics- Hierarchical, appointments are important, business cards are exchanged.

Literacy- 98.5%

Economy- High income

GDP- $37,900

Regulation- Mostly egal investment.

Cryptocurrency- Binanace, Kraken, Bitpanda are the cryptocurrency exchange platforms.

AUSTRIA:

Population- 8,940,860

Business Culture Characteristics- Meticulous attention, punctuality, dress code is formal.

Literacy- 99%

Economy- One of the strongest EU & Euro economies.

GDP- $54,100

Regulation- Mostly legal investment.

Cryptocurrency- Cryptocurrency is accepted. Binance, Kraken, Bitpanda are the cryptocurrency exchange platforms.

BELGIUM:

Population: 11,913,633

Business Culture Characteristics: Hierarchical, job titles & ranks are important, meetings are formal, decision-making is slow, appointments should be made in advance.

Literacy: 99%

Economy: High income economy

GDP: $51,700

Regulation: Mostly legal investment

Cryptocurrency: Legal. Cryptocurrency exchange platforms are: Uphold, Bybit, Binance, Bitpanda, Crypto.com

FINLAND:

Population: 5,614,571

Business Culture Characteristics: Informal work relationships, open communications & trust, mutual respect, punctuality.

Literacy: 100%

Economy: Highly industrialized, export-based

GDP: $49,600

Regulation: Mostly legal investment

Cryptocurrency: Cryptocurrency exchange platforms are: Binance, Kraken, Bitpanda

BULGARIA:

Population: 6,827,736

Business Culture Characteristics: Based on relationships & trust, business etiquette.

Literacy: 97%

Economy: Upper-middle-income

Regulation: Mostly legal investment

Cryptocurrency: Cryptocurrency exchange platforms are: Bybit, Binance, Uphold, BitStamp. Crypto.com

GREECE:

Population- 10,497,595

Business Culture Characteristics- Hierarchical structure

Literacy- 97.9%

Economy- Tourism & shipping

GDP- $29,500

Regulation- Mostly legal investment.

Cryptocurrency- Cryptocurrency exchange platforms are: Binance, Kraken, Bitpanda are the cryptocurrency exchange platforms.

NORWAY:

Population- 5,597,924

Business Culture Characteristics- Non-hierarchical, quite informal, values independence.

Literacy- 100%

Economy- High income. Large state-owned energy companies,

GDP- $65,700

Regulation- Mostly legal investment.

Cryptocurrency- The cryptocurrency exchange platforms are Binance, Kraken, Bitpanda.

SWEDEN:

Population- 10,536,338

Business Culture Characteristics- Based on egalitarism, professionalism, punctuality & work-life balance.

Literacy- 99%

Economy- Small, open, competitive & thriving economy.

GDP- $53,600

Regulation- Mostly legal investment.

Cryptocurrency- Cryptocurrency exchange platforms are: Binance, Kraken, Bitpanda are the cryptocurrency exchange platforms.

CYPRUS:

Population- 1,308,120

Business Culture Characteristics- Punctuality, trust, personal relationships.

Literacy- 99%

Economy- Service-based, high income

GDP- 41,700

Regulation- Mostly legal investment.

Cryptocurrency- Cryptocurrency is accepted. Cryptocurrency exchange platforms are: eToro, Kraken, Uphold, OKX, KuCoin.

MOROCCO:

Population: 37,067,420

Business Culture Characteristics- Hierarchical, interpersonal relationships.

Literacy- 75%

Economy- Lower-middle-income, tourism.

GDP- $8,100

Regulation- Mostly legal investment.

Cryptocurrency- Cryptocurrency exchange platforms are: Bybit, Kraken, OKX, Gate.io, KuCoin

IRAN:

Population: 87,590,873

Business Culture Characteristics: Meeting punctuality, business relationships.

Literacy: 88.7%

Economy: State-controlled economy

GDP: $15,000

Regulation: Mostly legal investment

Cryptocurrency: International payments allowed. Cryptocurrency exchange platforms are: Nobitex, Wallex.ir, Excoino, Aban Tether, Bit24.cash

NETHERLANDS:

Population- 17,463,930

Business Culture Characteristics- Business communications, hierarchical.

Literacy-99%

Economy- High income

GDP- $56,600

Regulation- Mostly legal investment.

Cryptocurrency- Cryptocurrency exchange platforms are: eToro, crypto.com, BitStamp, Coinbase, Bitvaro, LiteBit

DENMARK:

Population- 5,946,984

Business Culture Characteristics- Teamwork, open communication, flexible business hours

Literacy-99%

Economy- Diversified EU-trade-based economy.

GDP- $58,000

Regulation- Mostly legal investment.

Cryptocurrency- Cryptocurrency exchange platforms are: Bybit, Capital, Binance, Plus500, Bitpanda, Uphold, Arabase

LUXEMBOURG:

Population- 660,924

Business Culture Characteristics- Punctuality, politeness.

Literacy- 100%

Economy- High income

GDP- $115,700

Regulation- Mostly legal investment.

Cryptocurrency- Cryptocurrency exchange platforms are: eToro, BitStamp, Binance, Uphold.

ICELAND:

Population: 360,872

Business Culture Characteristics: Everyone is treated equally, friendliness, personal relationships.

Literacy: 99%

Economy: High income

Regulation: Mostly legal investment

Cryptocurrency: Legal. Cryptocurrency exchange platforms are: Binance, Krake, Bitpanda

PORTUGAL:

Population- 10,223,150

Business Culture Characteristics- Characterized by a strong emphasis on building relationships, hierarchical structure punctuality.

Literacy-96%

Economy- High income, tourism.

GDP- $33,700

Regulation- Mostly legal investment.

Cryptocurrency- Cryptocurrency exchange platforms are: Uphold, Bitpanda, Bybit, eToro, Binance.

U.S.A:

Population- 339,665,118

Business Culture Characteristics- There are different segments in the population based on demographic and psychographic parameters. The US has inhabitants with origins from all parts of the world with the majority of the population being of European descent. Hispanics (Latinos) and African Americans (Black) constitute the largest minority population in the country. In terms of geography, the majority of the population in the US lives in urban areas with many of those being in suburban areas. There are also several regional differences that exist in the US in terms of dialect and colloquial behavior. There are four regions in the US and fifty states, with each having its own nuances and social norms. For almost all cultures, it is important to understand how executives view power and authority. Many US managers are highly individualistic, time-conscious, goal-oriented people. In most cases, the manager is accountable for all decision-making that they are responsible for. Open dialogue is often welcomed in regard to debate and discussing business matters. In addition, communication can be very direct and to the point in order to move business along. The primary purpose of communication is to exchange information, facts, and opinions. Establishment of a personal relationship is not as important in US business culture. Instead, forming business relationships are deemed more important. However, the act of networking, or building relationships for future opportunities, is often viewed as a vital component to individual advancement. Meetings tend to be formal, with the aim being to solidify a business deal versus cultivating a personal connection. Although cordial exchanges, politeness, and small talk upon introduction are common, these should be viewed as protocol. Other protocols include adhering to meeting times and deadlines, obeying organization structure and hierarchy, and following business policies.

Literacy- 92%

Economy- Higher income, larger importer & second larger exporter

GDP per capita- $63,700

Regulations- Mostly legal investment.

Cryptocurrency- Cryptocurrency exchange platforms are: Kraken, eToro, Uphold, BinanceUS, Coinbase.

CANADA:

Population- 38,516,736

Business Culture Characteristics- Canadians Re formal as compared to the Americans. The culture in Canada is so markedly influenced by Europeans norms that it becomes imperative for business people to address the region separately. Diversity, cultural differences, conservative, politeness, respect.

Literacy- 99%

Economy- One of the world's largest economies, U.S trade partner.

GDP- $47,900

Regulations- Mostly legal investment. Bitcoin is considered a commodity for income tax purposes by the Canada Revenue Agency. Any income's Canadian's receives from a cryptocurrency sale or exchange must be reported as business income or a capital gain. Cryptocurrency exchanges are considered money service businesses and must be registered with Financial Transactions and Report Analysis Centre of Canada.

Cryptocurrency- Cryptocurrency is accepted. Cryptocurrency exchange platforms are: Bitbuy, virgoCX, wealthsimple, crypto, netcoins, newton, coinsmart, coinbase.

MEXICO:

Population- 128,649,565

Business Culture Characteristics- The Mexicans are seen to be hospitable and warm group of people. Mexican attitude and behavior tend to be a combination of both European and Native American influences. To the Mexican, the uniqueness of the individual should be recognized. The family plays a chief role in an average Mexican's life, and emphasis is placed on knowing one's family ties and connection prior to conducting business with them. Family relationships tend to be the basis upon which bonds are established and fostered. It is necessary for the foreign business to understand that questions posed regarding family are a means of ascertaining their well-being rather than an intrusion into privacy. Most Mexicans speak in a circulatory manner and often avoid any direct references or conversation. In order to ensure that there is a pleasant atmosphere, Mexicans will tell their counterparts what they would want to hear, rather than mention anything harsh. This is not to say that they knowingly flatter in order to get their work done, the purpose is often to please the other party and to make them feel at home. When approaching the organizational structure, it is important to note the hierarchy within the business. The top-down system is very much in effect and seniority is considered to be aa discriminating factor between levels. It is advisable for the foreign concern to be aware of the ranking of officials and alter its decision-making style based on hierarchical differentiation. One major aspect to note is machismo – the concept of masculinity that infiltrates into business dealings as well. Though women are represented in several managerial positions, it is believed that only a man should earn the respect from society and demonstrate leadership qualities.

Literary- 95.2%

Economy- One of the largest economies, Manufacturing sector.

GDP- $19,100

Regulation- Mostly legal investment.

Cryptocurrency- Cryptocurrencies are considered as commodities. Cryptocurrency exchange pltforms are: Bybit, Karken, Gate.io

UNITED KINGDOM:

Population- 68,138,484

Business Culture Characteristics- Characterized by courtesy, politeness, discipline, punctuality & ironic humor.

Literacy- 99%

Economy- Higher income & sixth larger importer & second larger exporter

GDP per capita- $45,000

Regulation- Mostly legal investment.

Cryptocurrency- Cryptocurrency exchange platforms are: OKX, Bybit, Binance, Coinbase, KuCoin.

CAYMAN ISLANDS:

Population: 65,483

Business Culture Characteristics: Influence by Afro-Caribbeans.

Literacy: 99%

Economy: Dominant offshore banking

GDP: $67,500

Regulation: Virtual assets are accepted.

Cryptocurrency: Cryptocurrency exchange platforms are: Roboforex, AvaTrade, FPmarkets, XTB Trading, Pepperstone, eToro.

UNITED ARAB EMIRATES (UAE):

Population- 9,973,449

Business Culture Characteristics- Multi-cultural society, hierarchical, social networking, personal relationships.

Literacy- 95.5%

Economy- Oil-driven economy.

GDP per capita- $69,700

Regulations- Mostly legal investment.

Cryptocurrency- Their government documents and systems are on the blockchain. They estimated that its blockchain has the potential to save 25.1 million hours in productivity. They have a Global Blockchain Council (GBC) with seven public – private collaborations, combining the skills and resources of startups, local businesses, and government departments -Healthcare, The diamond trade, Title transfers, Business registration, Tourism, Shipping.

Cryptocurrency exchange platforms are: Binance, OKX, Kraken, Bybit, Gate.io

SAUDI ARABIA:

Population- 35,939,806

Business Culture Characteristics- The majority of the population in Saudi Arabia is native to the country, with foreigners from the Middle east, Africa, and other countries comprising the remainder. Most of the population, including the traditionally nomadic population, has settled in the major cities throughout the country. One-fourth of the population has origins from the Bedouin people, the majority of nomadic population in the region, who hold a prominent position in the society. Saudi Arabia, as defined by Saudi Law, is a Muslim nation, with Islam being the only recognized religion. The majority of residents, about 90%, are Sunni Muslims who follow the Salafism Islamic code, and 5% of the population are Shia Muslims. Beyond the stereotyping that all Arabs are Muslims, what is essential to note is that the religion complements the Arab way of life. Arab means pertaining to Arabia and carries with it the cultural connotation and not the religious association. Saudi Arabians tend to perceive business to be a means to gain understanding of the Middle Eastern methods of management. Time is a major commodity, but patience is a virtue. It is beneficial for the foreign party to spend time in getting accustomed to Arab culture. Arabs are considered to be people of great emotional depth who believe in expressing their loyalty and friendship as key to an ongoing relationship. In conducting business, they tend to be warm, hospitable, and when the party becomes more aware of the nuances of the culture, makes it a very easy-going discussion. The concept of the individual is very important in Arab culture. One cannot afford to lose face or ruin his family's name in the process of dealing with others. There is a hierarchy in society, whether stipulated or otherwise, and an individual who has been shamed loses his status in the eyes of the group. Negotiating is considered to be part of the average business deal and one should ideally expect that it will take time for a unanimous decision to be reached.

Literacy- 97.5%

Economy- High income, oil-based economy.

GDP per capita- $44,300

Regulation- Mostly legal investment.

Cryptocurrency- Cryptocurrency exchange platforms are: Binance, Bybit, Rain, OKX, Gate.io

GLOSSARY

Altcoin: Any cryptocurrency that is an alternative to Bitcoin.

Bitcoin: The first decentralized cryptocurrency released in 2009.

Blockchain: A type of decentralized public digital ledger which contains block / records / transactions and form the basis for how many cryptocurrencies work, using cryptography link together blocks / records / transactions in a chain so that each block / record / transaction is linked with the previous one chronologically, preventing any tampering or revisionist history from occurring since it would be recognized immediately by other users on the network.

Centralized: A system of power where a central authority has control over the execution of operations. Often associated with a dictator style of rules and a single point of attack.

Cryptocurrency: A form of digital asset that uses cryptography as its main security measure to control the creations of additional units and verify transactions on its decentralized network.

Cryptography: The use of cryptographic protocols or mathematical techniques to encrypt messages sent between parties which are then decrypted using a key for security purposes.

Decentralized: When something does not have any central control but rather operates independently through per-to-peer network and consensus algorithms instead, transactions cannot be reversed once confirmed on blockchains that do not have any central authority or place of residence since they are decentralized.

Decentralized applications (DApps): Decentralized applications are essentially software programs built and hosted on blockchain technology, providing users with various functions through per-t-peer action rather than depending upon traditional intermediaries such as government or bank. Decentralized applications are frequently used to execute decentralized finance (DeFi) operations.

Decentralized Autonomous Organization (DAO): A cryptocurrency or business that is run by 'smart contracts' and governed by its token-holding community.

Decentralized Exchange (DEX): A system that allows for the trustless, peer-to-peer trading of cryptocurrencies without a third party or intermediary trading fees along the way.

Decentralized Finance (DeFi): It pushed the development of alternative decentralized blockchain-based financial applications without third parties. Decentralized finance applications include lending platforms, exchanges, prediction markets and many more solutions built on top of various protocols such as Ethereum or Bitcoin.

Distributed Digital Ledger (DLT): A type of database that is spread out across several nodes in different locations and countries so that it can remain decentralized as well as transparent to those involved with keeping records on it. Every single node will hold a complete copy which is updated regularly through consensus algorithms when new transactions take place. This allows for faster processing speeds since multiple copies are already available rather than one central authority who has to distribute them from scratch if something does go wrong.

Ethereum: Ethereum is like bitcoin in that it offers digital cash freed from the interference of governments, banks and credit cards. It furnishes blockchain infrastructure that does more than just allow people to make transactions with cryptocurrency. There are a number of Ethereum-based applications available. They include smart contracts which are written in code and execute themselves. Some of the contracts support decentralized finance (DeFi), a process that eliminates the need for brokerages and other third parties in financial transactions. Ethereum supports NFTs [Non- Fungicide Token], which represent the ownership of something, either real or digital. The platform supports the development of other currencies.

Ethereum Virtual Machine (EVM): It helps to run 'smart contract' on Ethereum's blockchain by keeping track of their state and allowing them to be executed simultaneously across their network through consensus.

Exchange: Platforms that allow users to buy, sell, or trade cryptocurrencies for other digital currency or traditional currencies such as US dollar or euros.

Fiat Currency: A legal tender declared by the government. This can be backed by its economy and has an institution that regulates it (central bank). For example- British Pound (GBP) & US Dollar (USD).

Hash: A specific algorithm that maps data of any size to a fixed size output.

Initial Coin Offering [ICO]: If anyone or a group wants to launch a new cryptocurrency, they need funds to develop their software, or they just want to turbocharge trading in the new coin.

Meme coin: A digital currency that doesn't have any inherent value and is used for social media purposes.

Mining: The process of creating new cryptocurrency units by solving complex mathematical problems, which are then verified and added to the blockchain.

Non-Fungible-Tokens (NFT): Digital assets which are unique and can't be replaced by generic items like coins.

Node: A connected computer that is part of a network, Blockchain in this case. All nodes are equal, and each one can be used to broadcast messages across the entire system.

Peer-to-peer: A system where two parties can conduct financial transactions with each other without involving a third party, like a bank. The blockchain is an example of this since it connects nodes in its network directly to one another and allows them to share data / transactions freely between themselves.

Public key: A cryptographic key that allows a user to receive cryptocurrency from another user but cannot be used to send funds. It usually consists of 64 characters to encrypt your wallet or make digital signatures.

Private key: A cryptographic key that allows users to send cryptocurrency from their wallet but cannot be used to receive funds. It usually consists of 64 characters which you use for decrypting your wallet or making digital signatures.

Smart contract: A piece of code that is executed on the blockchain after certain conditions have been met. This allows developers to create decentralized applications without having to build their blockchains from scratch.

Stable coin: A cryptocurrency designed to minimize price volatility, usually by pegging its value or supply against a physical asset such as fiat currencies like US Dollar.

Token: Token is a digital representation of an asset or utility that resides on a blockchain network. It can be created, transferred and owned by participants within the network. A unit value used for various purposes within a crypto ecosystem. Tokens can represent any cryptocurrencies.

Tokenization: It works by creating a digital token that represents an asset, such as currency. This token is then stored on a blockchain, which is a decentralized digital ledger that can be used to store and transfer data in a secure transparent way.

Transactional fee: The sum of money paid to miners to confirm transactions into blocks and add them to the blockchain network.

Wallet: A digital location used to store crypto funds by storing private and public keys that provide access to your cryptocurrency holdings.

BIBILIOGRAPHY / REFERENCES

Agur, Itai, Anil Ari, and Giovanni Dell' Ariccia. 2021. 'Designing Central Bank Digital Currencies.' Journal of Monetary Economics.'

Andolfatto, David. 2021. 'Assessing the Impact of Central Bank Digital Currency on Central Banks.' Economic Journal 131, no. 634: 525-540.

Arvidsson, Nikolas. 2019. Building a Cashless Society: 'Swedish Route to the Future of Cash Payments. Springer Briefs in Economics. Cham, Switzerland: springer Nature.

Aslanidis, Nektarios, Aurelio F. Bariviera, and Oscar Martinez-Ibafiez. 2019. 'An Analysis of Cryptocurrencies Conditions Cross Correlations,' 'Finance Research Letters 31, 130-137.

Auer, Raphael, and Rainer Boehme. 2020. 'The Technology of Retail Central Bank Digital Currency.' BIS Quarterly Review (March): 85-100.

Bank of Canada, European Central Bank, Bank of Japan, Sveriges Riksbank, Swiss National Bank, Bank of England, Board of Governors of the Federal Reserve, and bank of International Settlements. 2020. Central Bank Digital Currencies: Foundational Principles and Core Features. Bank for International Settlements. https://www.bis.org/pub/othp33.pdf.

Bank of England. 2020. 'Central Bank Digital Currency Opportunities, Challenges and Design.' Bank of England. https://

www.bankofengland.co.uk/-/media/boe/files/paper/2020/central-bank-digital-currency-opportunities-challenges-and-design.pdf.

Bano. Shehar, Alberto Sonnino, Mustafa Al-Bassam, Sarah Azouvi, Patrick McCorry, Sarah Meilkejohn, and George Danezis. 2019. SoK: Consensus in the Age of Blockchains.

Barrdear, John, and Michael Kumhof, 2016. 'The Microeconomics of Central Bank-Issued Digital Currencies.' Bank of England.

Bech, Morten Linneman, and Rodney Garratt. 2017. 'Central Bank Cryptocurrencies.' Bank for International Settlement Quarterly Review. pp. 55-70.

Bergara, Mario, and Jorge Ponce. 2018. 'Central Bank Digital Currency: The Uruguayan e-Peso Case. 'Unpublished manuscript, Central Bank of Uruguay, Montevideo.

Bonneau, Joseph, Andrew Miller, Jeremy Clark, Arvind Narayanan, Joshua Kroll, and Edward W. Felten. 2015. 'Research Perspectives and Challenges for Bitcoin and Cryptocurrencies.'

Bordo, Michael D., and Andrw T. Levin. 2017. 'Central Bank digital Currency and the future of Monetary Policy.'

Brainard, Lael, 2018. 'Cryptocurrencies, Digital Currencies, and Distributed Ledger Technologies: What Are We learning?'

Brunnermeier, Markus K., Harold James, and Jean-Pierre Landau, 2029. 'The Digitalization of Money.'

Camara, Noelia, Enestor Dos Santos, Francisco Grippa, Javier Sebastian, Fernando Soto., and Cristina Varela. 2018. 'Central Bank Digital Currencies: An assessment of Their Adoption in Latin America.

Carstens, Agustin. 2018. 'Money in the Digital Age: What Role for Central Banks?'

Casey, Michael, and Joshua S. Gans. 2019. 'Initial Coin Offerings and the Value of Crypto Tokens.'

Chen, Kaiji, Jue Ren, and Tao Zha. 2018. 'The Nexus of Monetary Policy and Shadow Banking in China.' American Economic Review 108, no. 12 pp. 3891-3936.

Clark, John, Nathan Converse, Brahima Coulibaly, and Steven Kamin. 2019. 'Emerging Market Capital Flows and U.S. Monetary Policy,' International Finance 23, no.1 pp. 2-17.

Coeure, Benoit, 2019. 'Digital Challenges to the International Monetary and Financial system.'

Collomb, Alexis, Primavera De Filippi, and Klara Sok. 2019. 'Blockchain Technology and Financial Regulation: A Risk-Based Approach to the Regulation of ICOs.' European Journal of Risk Regulation 10, no. 2: pp 263-314.

Cong, Lin William, and Zhiguo He. 2019. 'Blockchain Disruption and Smart Contracts.' Review of Financial Studies 32, no. 5: pp. 1754-1797.

Conti, Mauro, Sandeep Kumar E., Chhagan Lal, and Sushimita Ruj. 2017. 'A Survey on Security and Privacy Issues of Bitcoin.' Institute of Electrical and Electronic Engineers.

Corbae, Dean, and Pablo D'Erasmo, 2020. 'Rising Bank Concentration. 'Journal of Economic Dynamic and Control.

Dain, Philip, Steven Goldfeder, Tyler Kell, Yungxi Li, Xueyuan Zhao, Iddo Bentov, Laurence Breidenbach, and Ari Jules, 2019. 'Front running, Transacting Reordering, and Consensus Instability in Decentralized Exchanges.'

Danezis, George, and Sarah Meiklejohn. 2016. 'Central Banked Cryptocurrencies.'

Demirguc-Kunt, Asli, Leora Klapper, Dorothy Singer, Saniya Ansar, and Jake Hess, 2018, Global Findex Database 2017: Measuring Financial Inclusion and the Fintech Revolution.

Dhawan, Anirudh, and Talis J. Putnins, 2020. 'A New Wolf in Town Pump and Dump Manipulation in Cryptocurrency Markets.'

Easley, David, Maureen O'Hara, and Soumya Basu. 2019. 'From Mining to Markets: The Evolution of Bitcoin Transaction Fees.' Journal of Financial Economics 134, no. pp 91-109.

Engert, Walter, and Ben S. C. Fung, 2017. 'Central Bank Digital Currency: Motivations and Implications.'

Fernandez-Villaverde, Jesus, Daniel Sanches, Linda Schilling, and Harald Uhlig, 2020. 'Central Bank Digital Currency.

Foley, Sean, Jonathan R. Karlsen, and Talis J. Putnins, 2019. 'Sex, Drugs, and Bitcoin: How Much Illegal Activity is Financed through Cryptocurrencies.' Review of Financial Studies 32, no. 5: pp 1798-1853.

Fung, Be S.C., and Hanna Halaburda 2016. 'Central Bank Digital Currencies: A Framework for Assessing Why and How.'

Garratt, Rodney, and Neil Wallace. 2018. 'Bitcoin 1, Bitcoin2,… 'An Experiment in Privately Issued Outside Monies.' Economic Inquiry 56, no. 3: pp 1887-1897.

Goldberg, Linda S. 2010. 'Is the International Role of the Dollar Changing?' Economics and Finance.

Goldstein, Itay, Wei Jiang, and G. Andrew Karolyi, 2019. 'To FinTech and Beyond.' Review of Financial Studies 32, no. 5: pp 1647-1661.

Griffin, John M., and Amin Shams. 2020. 'Is Bitcoin Really Un-tethered?' Journal of Finance 75, no. 4: pp 1775-2321.

Grimmelmann, James. 2019. 'All Smart Contracts Are Ambiguous.' Journal of Law and Innovation 2, no. 1: pp 1-22.

Grym, Aleksi. 2020. 'Lessons Learned from the World's First CBDC.' Bank of Finland Economics Review, no. 8: pp 1-22.

Howell, Sabrina, Marina Niessner, and David Yermack. 2021. 'Initial Coin Offerings: Financing Growth with Cryptocurrency Sales,' Review of Financial Studies.

Ingves, Stefan. 2017. 'Do We Need an e-Krona?'

Ismail, Leila, and Huned Materwala. 2019. 'A review of Blockchain Architecture and Consensus Protocols: Use Cases, Challenges, and Solutions.' Symmetry 11, no. 10: 1198.

Ju, Lan, Timothy Lu, and Zhiyong Tu. 2016. 'Capital Flight and Bitcoin Regulation.' International Review of Finance 16, no. 3: pp 445-455.

Mancini-Griffoli, Tommaso, Maria Soledad Martinez Peria, Itai Agur, John Kiff, Adina Popescu, and Celine Rochon. 2018. 'Casting Light on Central Bank Digital Currency.'

Massad, Timothy. 2019. 'It's time to Strengthen the Regulation of Crypto-Assets.'

Mora, Camilo, Randi L. Rollins, Katie Taladay, Micheal B. Kantar, Mason K. Chock, Niuo Shimada, and Erik C. Franklin. 2018. 'Bitcoin Emissions Alone Could Push Global Warming above 2 degrees Centigrade.' Nature Climate Change 8, no. 11: pp 931-933.

Narayanan, Arvind, Joseph Bonneau, Edward Felten, Andrew Miller, and Steven Goldfeder. 2016. Bitcoin and Cryptocurrency Technologies: A Comprehensive Introduction, Princeton, NJ: Princeton University Press.

Qiu, Tanh, Ruidong Zhang, and Yuan Gao. 2019. 'Ripple versus SWIFT: Transforming Cross Border Remittance Using Blockchain Technology.'

Raskin, Max, and David Yermack. 2018. "Digital Currencies, Decentralized Ledgers, and the Future of Central Banking.'

Schilling, Linda, and Harald Uhlig, 2018. 'Some Simple Bitcoin Economics.'

Schneider, John. 2017. FinTech and Financial Innovation: Drivers and Depth.

Stoll, Christian, Lena Klaasen, and Ulrich Gallersdorfer. 2019. 'The Carbon Footprint of Bitcoin.' Joule 3, no. 7: pp 1647-1661.

Vigna, Paul, and Michael Casey. 2016. The Ag of Cryptocurrency: How Bitcoin and Blockchain Are Changing the World Economic Order. New York: Picador.

Yao, Qian, 2017. 'The Application of Digital Currency in Interbank Cash Transfer Scenario.' Finance Computerizing 5: pp 16-19.

Printed in the United States
by Baker & Taylor Publisher Services